Exploring Our Solar System

SALLY RIDE AND TAM O'SHAUGHNESSY

CROWN PUBLISHERS ♛ NEW YORK

This book is dedicated to our readers—
the next generation of dreamers and doers.

Published by Crown Publishers, an imprint of Random House Children's Books,
a division of Random House, Inc., New York.
CROWN and colophon are trademarks of Random House, Inc.

www.randomhouse.com/kids

Library of Congress Cataloging-in-Publication Data
Ride, Sally.
Exploring our solar system / Sally Ride, Tam O'Shaughnessy.
p.   cm.
SUMMARY: Describes what we have learned about our solar system from telescopes and spacecraft,
focusing on the characteristics of the planets and their moons.
ISBN 0-375-81204-0 (trade) — ISBN 0-375-91204-5 (lib. bdg.)
1. Solar system—Juvenile literature. [1. Planets. 2. Solar system.]
I. O'Shaughnessy, Tam E. II. Title.
QB501.3 .R53 2003
523.2—dc21   2002017471

MANUFACTURED IN CHINA
November 2003
10 9 8 7 6 5 4 3 2
First Edition

Contents

Preface

When I was orbiting Earth in the space shuttle, I could float over to a window and gaze down at the delicate white clouds, brilliant orange deserts, and sparkling blue waters of the planet below. I could see coral reefs in the oceans, fertile farmlands in the valleys, and twinkling city lights beneath the clouds. Even from space, it is obvious that Earth is a living planet.

Earth would have looked very different to an astronaut four billion years ago. Blue water filled different oceans, thunderclouds hid nameless continents, and the barren land showed no signs of life.

Further back in time, five billion years ago,

a starship passing through our region of space would not have slowed down for a second look. There was nothing to see. No Earth, no Sun, no solar system. Nothing but a huge, tenuous cloud of gas. That cloud eventually contracted to form our Sun and all of its planets. Everything we know came from it.

Although the planets of our solar system all formed at about the same time and from about the same stuff, they are nine very different worlds. This book describes what we have learned about them from telescopes and spacecraft. It also describes our unique planet and how it is related to its neighbors in the solar system.

The Solar System: An Overview

When astronomers of ancient times charted the heavens, they found that a few of the twinkling lights wandered across the sky against the background of stars. They called them "planets," which is from the Greek word for "wanderers." Many hundreds of years later, scientists painstakingly plotted the paths of the planets across the sky. They learned that they, like Earth, orbit around the Sun.

The Sun, the center of our solar system, sits in the middle of a huge disk. The planets lie in the disk, and they all travel in the same direction as they circle the Sun. Many of the planets have moons that circle them just as the planets circle the Sun.

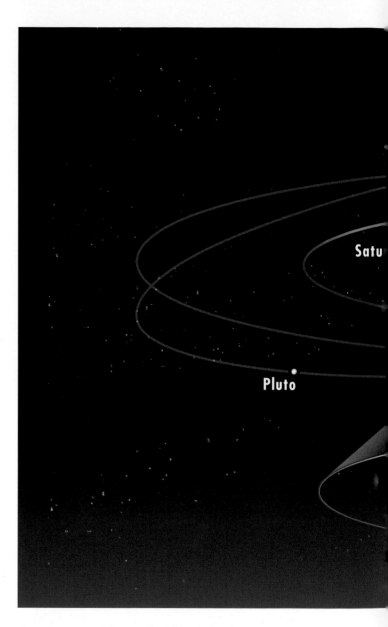

Our solar system, showing the orbits of the planets. As you move out from the Sun, the distance between the planets increases. The orbits and sizes of the planets are not to scale.

Artist's painting of the Milky Way galaxy as seen from above. It shows our galaxy's spiral arms, with a bright yellow dot representing our Sun.

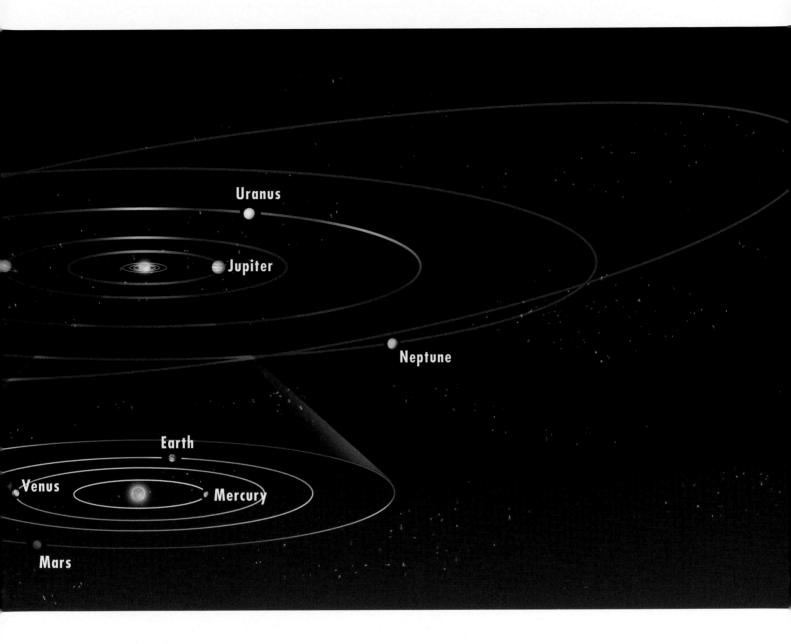

The Sun is a star. It is similar to billions of other stars in our galaxy. Although its size is typical for a star, the Sun is much, much bigger than anything else in our solar system—more than one million Earths would fit inside it.

The Sun, like other stars, is a shining ball of hot hydrogen and helium gas. The energy generated in its core is the source of light and heat in the solar system. We see the planets at night because they reflect the Sun's light—not because they generate light themselves.

Our Sun has nine planets in orbit around it. Although they are very different, they all orbit the Sun and are all big enough that their gravity pulled them into roughly spherical shapes.

The four planets closest to the Sun—Mercury, Venus, Earth, and Mars—are called the "terrestrial planets" because they are similar to Earth. (The word "terrestrial" is from the Latin word *terra*, which means "earth" or "land.") These worlds are relatively small, are made of rocky material, and have solid surfaces like Earth.

The next four planets are very different. These "giant planets"—Jupiter, Saturn, Uranus, and Neptune—are much larger than the terrestrial planets. They are made mostly of the lightest elements and don't have solid surfaces.

Pluto, the ninth planet, is small and icy; it is not like either the terrestrial planets or the giant planets.

There are billions of smaller bodies orbiting the Sun as well. Comets swing in very elongated orbits that take them near the Sun, then billions of miles away before they head back in. Thousands of rocky asteroids orbit between Mars and Jupiter, in a region appropriately called the Asteroid Belt. And thousands of small, icy bodies orbit the Sun in the cold, dark region beyond Neptune. This part of the disk is called the Kuiper Belt and these bodies are called Kuiper Belt Objects. The entire disk of the solar system is surrounded by the distant Oort Cloud, a swarm of icy bodies that extends nearly halfway to the nearest star.

Formation of the Solar System

Our solar system is shaped like a disk. The Sun is at the center, and the planets travel in near-circular paths around it. They all orbit in the direction that the Sun itself spins on its axis. This simple but elegant pattern hints that the Sun and planets share a common origin. They do. About 4.6 billion years ago, a cloud of interstellar gas collapsed to form a shining star and its family of planets.

Our Sun was formed with hundreds of other nearby stars in what astronomers call a stellar nursery. This cold cloud of gas, many light-years across, began to collapse under its own gravity. As it collapsed, it broke up into hundreds of smaller clouds. One of those clouds collapsed to form the beginnings of our solar system: an early star—our Sun—surrounded by a disk of gas that would produce its planets.

As the cloud contracted, its center grew denser and denser, and hotter and hotter, until it was dense enough and hot enough that its hydrogen atoms collided with enough energy to combine. This process of combining hydrogen to form helium is called "nuclear fusion." It releases enormous amounts of energy and produces the sunlight that bathes our solar system. The early Sun began to shine.

While the center of the cloud was collapsing to form the Sun, its outer fringes were pulled into a disk of gas and dust that swirled around it. The spinning disk was quite hot, especially near the young Sun. As it cooled, some of the gas and dust condensed into small solid particles. Occasionally, the particles collided and stuck together. Tiny clumps quickly grew to the size of baseballs, then boulders, then buildings. Once this started, the big just kept getting bigger and bigger.

Though the disk was made mostly of hydrogen and helium gas, the solid lumps grew out of microscopic bits of ice, rock, or metal. The composition of the lumps was determined by their distance from the Sun. Nearest the Sun, it was very hot—too hot for ice, so the lumps that grew in this part of the disk were made of rock and metal.

Soon, the inner part of our solar system was filled with hundreds of rocky objects the size of small moons. Over the next 100 million years, these "planetesimals" combined in a series of colossal collisions to form Mercury, Venus, Earth, and Mars.

Out beyond Mars, the disk was cool enough for ice to form. The solid particles that collided and grew contained both rock and ice. Jupiter, Saturn, Uranus, and Neptune would form from these icy planetesimals.

These distant planets suddenly began to grow faster because of changes in the early

The formation of our solar system.

Sun. During its transition to a stable star, the Sun blew a wind of high-energy particles into the disk around it. This wind swept the gas that was left in the disk toward the outer planets. As the gas was blown into the colder part of the solar system, some of it condensed into a blizzard of ice. Young Jupiter and Saturn quickly scooped it up, and each grew to about twenty times the size of present-day Earth. Once they became this large, their gravity was able to attract the hydrogen and helium gas around them, and they grew even bigger.

Uranus and Neptune were farther from the Sun and grew more slowly. Before they became large enough to attract the hydrogen and helium gas, most of it had already been blown out of the solar system. So these two planets became large, but not nearly as large as Jupiter and Saturn.

The asteroid Eros is only twenty-one miles long. (*Near Earth Asteroid Rendezvous*)

Icy planetesimals also formed beyond Neptune. Here the gas was thinner and the distance between the icy rocks was greater, so they grew much more slowly. Thousands of those planetesimals are still out there today. These frigid relics of the early solar system are the Kuiper Belt Objects. Pluto, the smallest

Artist's paintings of the Kuiper Belt — the collection of icy objects in orbit around the Sun beyond Neptune. The top painting shows that the Kuiper Belt extends far beyond the planets. The bottom painting, an edge-on view, shows the Kuiper Belt is in the plane of the solar system.

WFPC2
Visible Light

This photograph shows the birth of stars in a nearby galaxy, the Large Magellanic Cloud. (*Hubble Space Telescope*)

and oddest of our planets, appears to be one of the largest members of this family.

All the planets formed quickly—in just the first 100 million years or so after the disk formed. But not all the planetesimals were gobbled up by the growing planets. Billions of these chunks of rock and ice were still flying around the solar system. Some bombarded the newly formed planets, occasionally colliding with enough force to change a planet forever. Thousands of the planetesimals between Mars and Jupiter might have formed another planet, but Jupiter was near enough that its gravity disrupted the planet-building process. These small rocky objects are still orbiting the Sun and are now known as "asteroids." Billions of planetesimals between Jupiter and Neptune were hurled out of the disk by the gravity of the giant planets. They now make up the vast, remote Oort Cloud that surrounds our solar system.

How do we know all this? Powerful telescopes now let us watch stars form in other parts of our galaxy and in neighboring galaxies. Although we can't watch a single cloud collapse to form a star and planets (that would take 100 million years!), we can study different stars at different stages of evolution. Astronomers have found huge clouds in the midst of collapse and young stars surrounded by disks of gas with gaps in them that may have been swept clean by growing planets.

We also have evidence about the birth of our own solar system. Comets and asteroids—leftover planetesimals—are relics of its earliest days. A very few small pieces have made their way to Earth and fallen to the ground as meteorites. They provide clues to the age of the solar system, the composition of the early cloud, and the conditions under which the planets formed. These remnants of the early solar system confirm that the Sun and its planets formed at the same time and from the same cold cloud of gas.

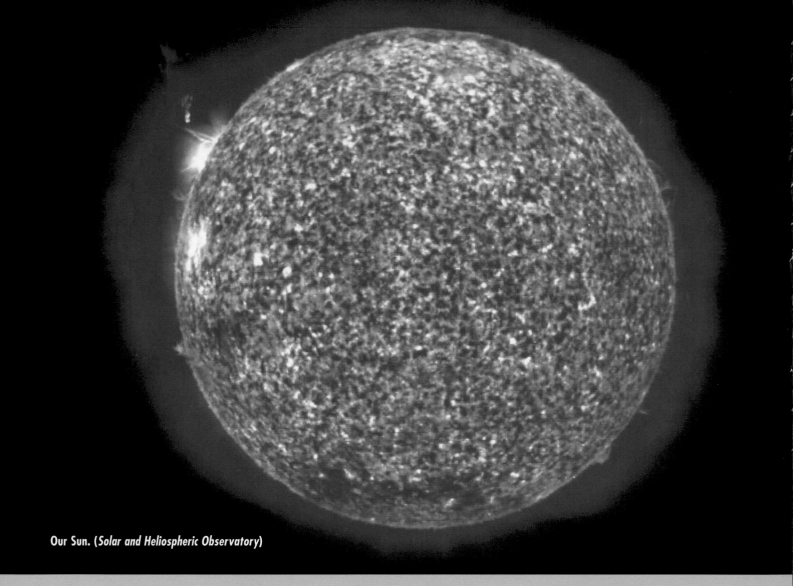

Our Sun. (*Solar and Heliospheric Observatory*)

The Sun

DIAMETER	**864,000 miles (110 x Earth's)**
MASS	**330,000 times Earth's**
TEMPERATURE	**27 million °F (center)**
	10,000 °F (surface)
ROTATION PERIOD	**25 days (equator) to 35 days (poles)**

The Sun is a glowing ball of very, very hot gas. It is made almost entirely of hydrogen and helium and is by far the largest object in the solar system. All the planets and their moons could easily fit inside a small corner of it. In fact, the Sun is about 99.9% of all the material in the solar system!

While Earth and the other planets are orbiting around it, the Sun itself is spinning on its axis like a top. Because it is made of gas all the way through, it spins faster at the equator than at the poles. The Sun's equator rotates once every twenty-five Earth days; the polar regions about once every thirty-five Earth days.

This ball of 71% hydrogen and 27% helium is held together by its own gravity; it is kept from collapsing by the pressure exerted by the hot gas. At the Sun's center, the temperature reaches over 27 million degrees Fahrenheit, and the pressure is immense. Under these conditions, hydrogen atoms zip around at enormous speeds and smash into each other hard enough to combine, forming helium. This releases huge amounts of energy—the energy that powers the Sun. This energy slowly makes its way outward from the Sun's core. But it takes a very long time—several hundred thousand years—to travel from the heart of the Sun to its surface and finally escape as sunlight.

The Sun is unimaginably hot at its center and cools toward the surface. The "surface" isn't solid; it's just the outer layer of gas from which light escapes. All the light we see comes from this surface layer of gas, the *photosphere*.

The Sun *is just one of billions of stars in our galaxy. It is a fairly average star and not particularly special—except to us. The Sun powers our solar system, and from sunrise to sunset it dominates our sky and directs the daily rhythms of our lives.*

The temperature of the photosphere is about 10,000 degrees Fahrenheit—much cooler than the Sun's core, but still intensely hot.

Just above the photosphere is the Sun's atmosphere: first the *chromosphere,* then the very thin, very hot *corona.* The faint, wispy

Artist's cutaway painting, showing the layers of the Sun. Energy is released in the Sun's core, then slowly makes its way to the surface and is emitted as sunlight. The Sun's visible surface is called the photosphere. Sunspots (gray/orange) and solar prominences (yellow/orange) are shown on the surface.

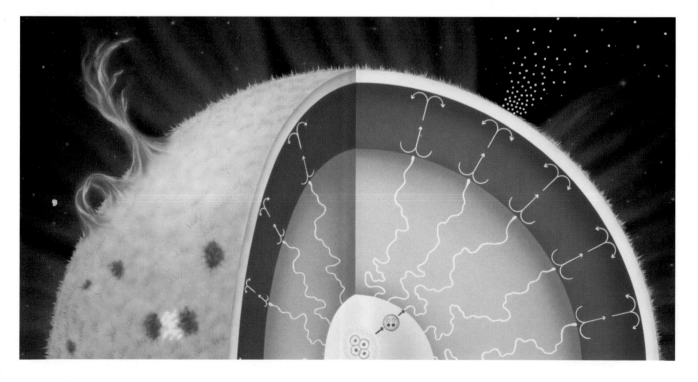

corona can be seen only during an eclipse, when the Moon passes in front of the Sun and blocks all of its bright light. At its farthest reaches, the corona turns into the *solar wind*—a stream of high-energy particles that blows outward through the entire solar system.

The Sun emits huge amounts of electromagnetic radiation, most of it in the form of visible light. Visible light is composed of all the colors of the rainbow, and it is the radiation that our eyes can detect. You might think it's a happy coincidence that the Sun emits exactly the type of light that we can see. But in fact, our eyes (and the eyes of most animals) have evolved in just the right way to enable them to detect the light that's available—the light from the Sun.

The Sun also emits much smaller amounts of other types of electromagnetic radiation: infrared light, ultraviolet light (the radiation that causes sunburn), radio waves, and even high-energy X-rays. But the lion's share of the energy it produces is radiated out into the solar system as visible light.

We often think of the Sun as a bright, yellow, unchanging ball. But telescopes and spacecraft have revealed an active, constantly changing star. Dark areas, called "sunspots," come and go on its surface. Sunspots are cooler areas on the blazing-hot photosphere. At times there are hundreds of them marking the surface; at other times there are none. Sunspots are caused by the Sun's changing magnetic field, but they are still not very well understood.

When the Sun is especially active, it can erupt violently. *Solar flares* are spectacular

The Sun's corona is visible only during a solar eclipse, when both the photosphere and the chromosphere are covered by the Moon. (NOAO)

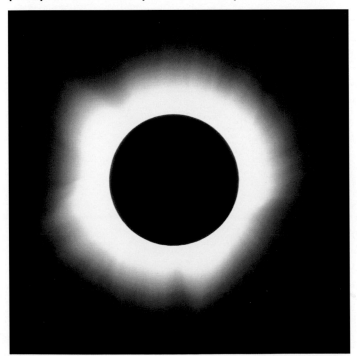

Several sunspots, including one large group, each about the size of Earth. Sunspots appear dark because they are slightly cooler than the surrounding photosphere. (*Solar and Heliospheric Observatory*)

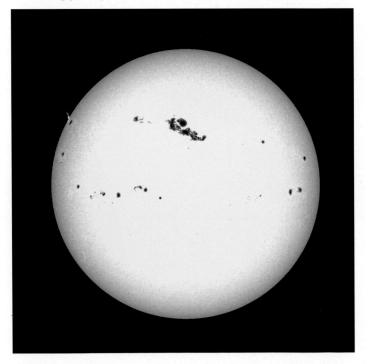

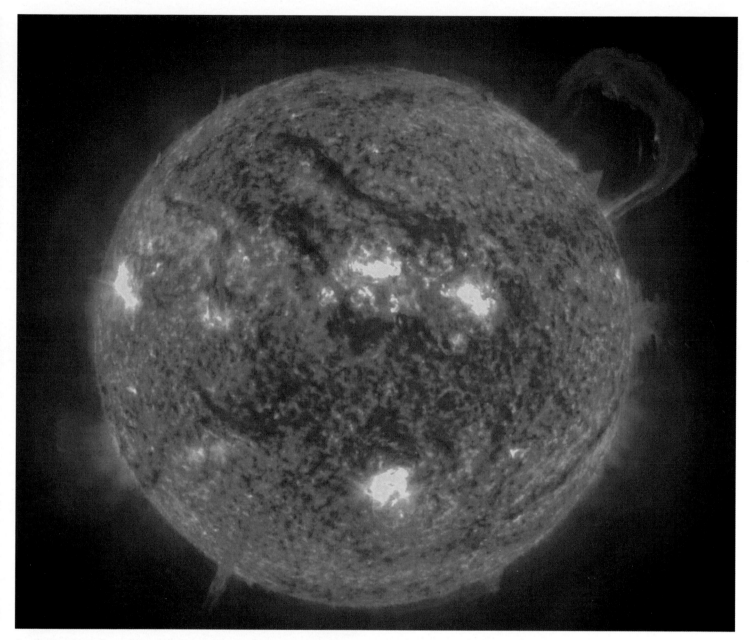

Sometimes the surface of the Sun erupts, releasing huge arcs of glowing gases that hover above the photosphere for days before collapsing to the surface. These are called solar prominences. The hottest areas appear bright yellow, while the darker areas indicate cooler temperatures. (*Solar and Heliospheric Observatory*)

explosions that flash across the surface in minutes, blasting particles into space. The particles streaming out from the Sun can cause power blackouts and disrupt communication signals 93 million miles away on Earth. Astronomers try to predict when solar flares are going to happen so that people can prepare for potential problems.

Our Sun has been shining for 4.5 billion years. During that time it has been burning the hydrogen in its central core. Eventually, the Sun's furnace will flicker out and this star will die. But that will not happen anytime soon! The Sun has enough fuel left to ensure that our planet will bathe in sunlight for about another five billion years.

The Terrestrial Planets

Mercury, Venus, Earth, and Mars—the four terrestrial planets—are small rocky worlds in the inner solar system. Earth is the biggest of the four; Mercury is the smallest. All these "inner planets" have solid surfaces that spacecraft could land on. All of them have lava-splashed land and mountains that cast shadows across the plains. All bask in the relative warmth of the nearby Sun.

The terrestrial planets formed about 4.5 billion years ago, from a flurry of rocky planetesimals in the inner part of the disk that surrounded the Sun. Hundreds of those planetary embryos crashed together to create the four planets.

The violent collisions heated and melted the young planets. At first, they were so hot that they were molten. Blobs of heavy elements, such as iron, settled to their centers and formed their cores. The iron cores were surrounded by molten rock.

Slowly, Mercury, Venus, Earth, and Mars began to cool. The outer skin of each cooled first, and soon each had a solid rocky crust. Their insides were still intensely hot. Volcanoes punched through their crusts and spread molten lava across the land.

The smaller a planet is, the faster it cools. Little Mercury cooled quickly. Soon, lava no longer rose to its surface. Mars kept its internal

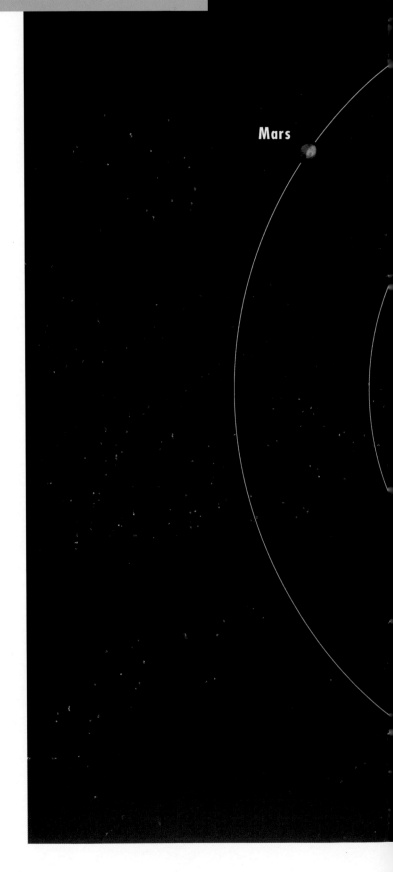

Mars

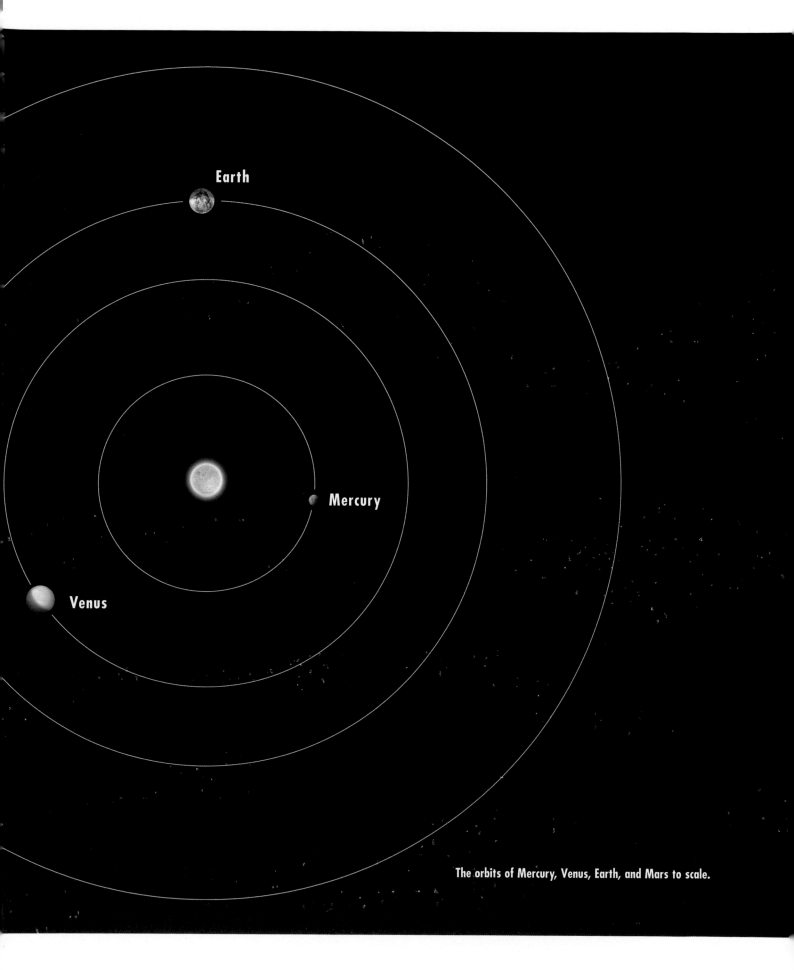

Earth

Mercury

Venus

The orbits of Mercury, Venus, Earth, and Mars to scale.

heat longer. Molten rock pushed up parts of the Martian land, and eruptions built the largest volcanoes in the solar system. Then Mars, too, eventually cooled, and its remaining internal heat does not have much effect on the planet today. In contrast, Venus and Earth are still hot and churning inside.

During the early days of the solar system, the planets were bombarded by leftover planetesimals. Mercury has thousands of craters from those collisions. So do the ancient highlands of Mars. Most of the craters on Venus and Earth have been erased—either covered over by lava or, on Earth, eroded by water or buried as the land is recycled.

The biggest collisions wreaked havoc. Mercury was hit by a huge object that stripped away much of its rocky outer layers. Venus was blasted by something big enough to nearly stop its rotation—it now spins very slowly, and backward. Earth was hit by an object the size of Mars. The impact ripped off part of Earth and formed our Moon.

As the planets cooled, gases bubbled out of

Mercury, Venus, Earth and its Moon, and Mars to scale.

the molten rock and formed their early atmospheres. Crashing comets and planetesimals added more water and ices. Mercury is small, so its gravitational pull is not as strong as those of the other terrestrial planets. It was not able to hold an atmosphere—most of its gases escaped to space. Venus, Earth, and Mars were large enough to hold on to the gases that surrounded them. Their early atmospheres were all made of carbon dioxide, nitrogen, and water vapor, but they have changed considerably over the years. The atmospheres of these three planets are now about as different as they can be.

The terrestrial planets started out as molten balls of rock, all created from the same swarm of planetesimals. But they were different distances from the Sun, different sizes, and evolved under different circumstances. Today, they are four very different worlds. Earth is the most remarkable. It is the only one with water on its surface, and—as far as we know—it is the only one with life.

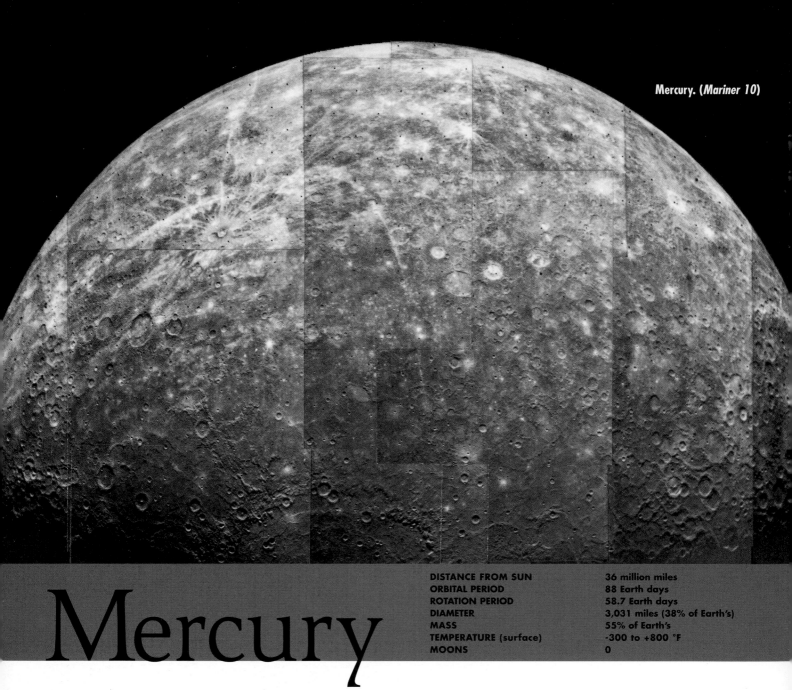

DISTANCE FROM SUN	36 million miles
ORBITAL PERIOD	88 Earth days
ROTATION PERIOD	58.7 Earth days
DIAMETER	3,031 miles (38% of Earth's)
MASS	55% of Earth's
TEMPERATURE (surface)	-300 to +800 °F
MOONS	0

Mercury

Mercury is difficult to study from Earth because it is inside Earth's orbit. An astronomer on our planet always has to look toward the Sun to find it. Mercury can only be seen just before sunrise or just after sunset, when the glare from the Sun doesn't obscure our view of it. Even under the best conditions, Mercury is not visible for long—so even Earth's most powerful telescopes can't tell us much about it.

Mercury makes one complete orbit around the Sun every eighty-eight days. While it is traveling around the Sun, it is also spinning, or rotating, on its axis. For a long time the rotation rate of Mercury was unknown. Then, in the early 1960s, scientists used radar to bounce signals off the planet. The radar sent out pulses of radio waves. The pulses bounced off the surface of Mercury back toward Earth and were caught by the large radar antennas.

The change in the signals' frequency revealed Mercury's rotation.

Mercury rotates very slowly. It takes almost fifty-nine Earth days for it to spin on its axis just once. As it makes one trip around the Sun, Mercury rotates only one and a half times. At this rate, a typical spot on the planet is in sunlight for about three Earth months, then in darkness for three Earth months.

The intense sunlight bakes the daylight side of Mercury and sends the temperature soaring to 800 degrees Fahrenheit. But while the daylight side is sizzling hot, the dark side is freezing cold. Since Mercury has essentially no atmosphere, it begins losing its heat to space as soon as the Sun sets. The nighttime temperature drops quickly, plummeting to

Mercury, *the closest planet to the Sun, is the smallest of the terrestrial worlds. It is only slightly larger than our Moon. This tiny planet is an inhospitable place. It has no atmosphere, its ancient surface is covered with impact craters, and its temperature ranges from a scorching 800 degrees Fahrenheit to a frigid 300 degrees below zero Fahrenheit. Mercury is the terrestrial planet that we know the least about.*

Mercury orbits the Sun inside Earth's orbit. This means that it always appears near the Sun in our sky.

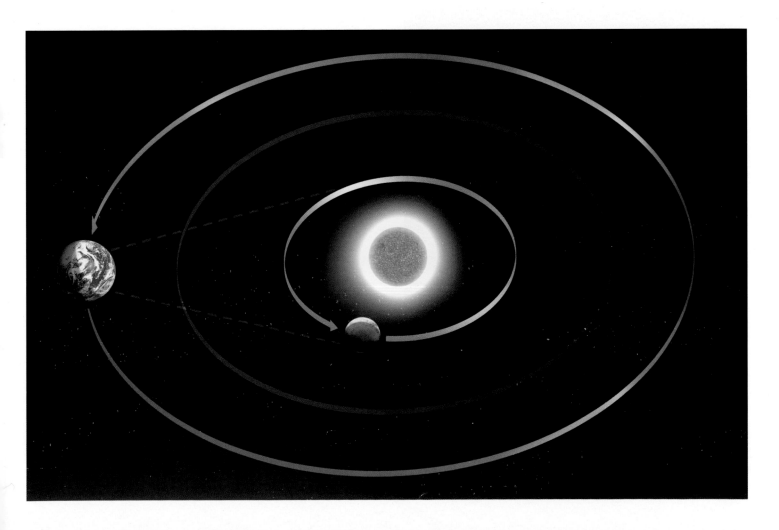

The Arecibo radio antenna in Puerto Rico. Radio waves, sent from large antennas such as Arecibo, bounce off Mercury and are received back on Earth. The signals that return provide information about the planet.

Artist's painting of *Mariner 10*, the only spacecraft to visit Mercury.

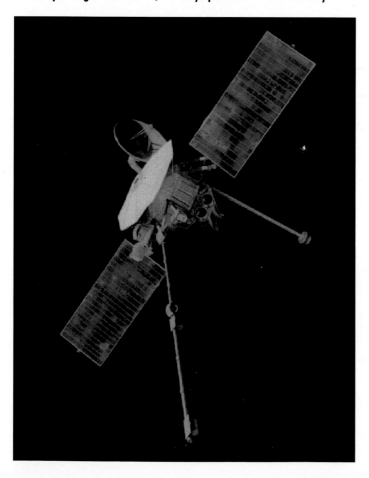

300 degrees below zero Fahrenheit during the long Mercury night. This difference in temperature (1,100 degrees Fahrenheit!) between the hottest and coldest points on the surface is greater on Mercury than on any other planet.

Only one spacecraft has been by Mercury, and its visits to the planet were a long time ago and very brief. In 1974 and 1975, *Mariner 10* flew past Mercury three times. It photographed less than half the planet, and only a tiny part of it in detail. No spacecraft has been back since.

Mariner 10 revealed a surface that is very old and probably hasn't changed much in almost four billion years. Mercury's surface is heavily cratered, with smooth volcanic plains between the craters. Everything is covered with a couple of inches of crushed rock — rock

One of the longest scarps on Mercury. It is about 220 miles long and in places almost two miles high. The scarp cuts a jagged path through a large crater. (*Mariner 10*)

that has been pulverized by the impact of meteor after meteor. The terrain is scratched with long scarps—cracks and ridges that are hundreds of miles long and over a mile high.

Some of Mercury's craters are huge. The Caloris Basin ("Basin of Heat") is about 800 miles across. It would stretch from California to the Rocky Mountains. The impact that formed this massive crater was so great that it sent shock waves through the planet, rattling and jumbling the land on the other side.

Mercury is a small planet. Only Pluto is smaller. In fact, Mercury is smaller than the largest moons of Jupiter and Saturn. However, when scientists analyzed the effect of Mercury's gravity on *Mariner 10,* they discovered that the little planet is surprisingly heavy for its size. Like the other terrestrial worlds, it has a

The huge impact that formed Mercury's Caloris Basin sent powerful shock waves all the way through the planet. The impact left the enormous crater and also created a large area of weird, hilly terrain on the other side of the world.

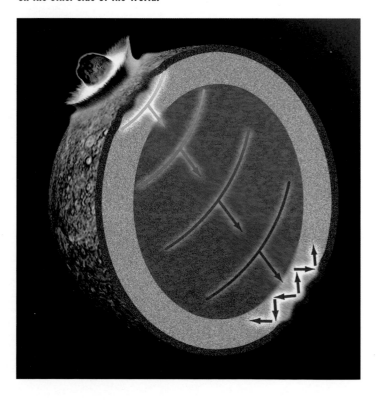

Mercury's core makes up a large part of the planet, as shown in this artist's painting.

solid iron core surrounded by rocky material and crust. But Mercury's iron core makes up an unusually large part of the planet. The core extends three-fourths of the way to the planet's surface. In comparison, Earth's core extends about halfway to its surface.

Mercury may once have had a much thicker rocky shell. It is very possible that the outer part of the planet was wrenched away when a huge planetesimal crashed into a young Mercury. The collision left the heavy iron core—but blasted away much of the rock that had surrounded it.

The Mercury we see today began to take shape after this colossal collision. Its young surface was pelted with smaller planetesimals,

The bright spots in this radar image are patches of ice around Mercury's north pole. The ice is inside craters in places where the crater rims cast permanent shadows.

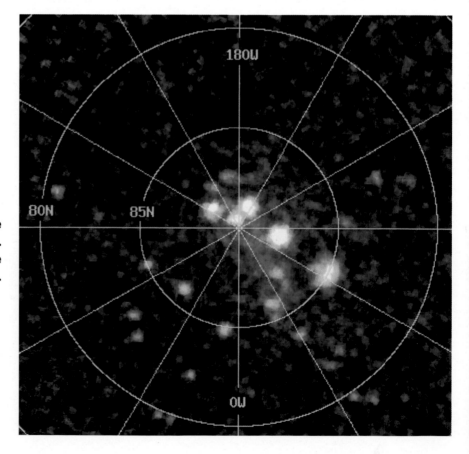

carving out the craters that still mark the planet today. At about the same time, molten rock beneath the surface was able to seep up through fissures, flow across the land, and form Mercury's volcanic plains.

As Mercury's inner core cooled, it shrank slightly. The surface above it cracked and sank in spots. This may be the origin of the long cracks and ridges that are found all over the planet.

If you landed on the surface of Mercury, you would find yourself on a place that looked very much like our Moon: a barren, airless world, with a gray dusty surface pockmarked by craters of all sizes. You would need a space-suit to survive.

The Sun, which you can easily block with your hand on Earth, is two and a half times bigger in Mercury's sky. A special gold visor on your helmet would have to protect your eyes from the glaring sunlight.

And the Sun would barely move across the sky. It would be visible for three months, slowly rising, reaching its peak, then slowly setting. For those three months, it would bake you in constant sunshine, heating the soil, the rocks, and your lander to unbearable temperatures.

Once the Sun set, you and your lander would be plunged into a long, cold night. A fuzzy yellow Venus and a pale blue Earth would be the brightest objects in the night sky.

Mercury's cratered surface. The planet's south pole is located inside the large crater. (*Mariner 10*)

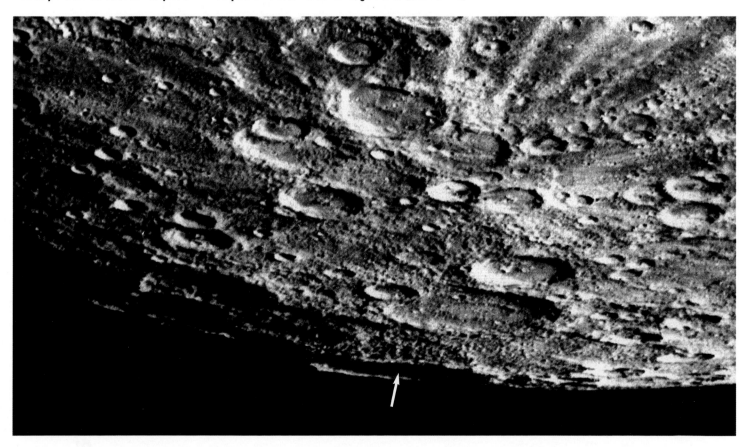

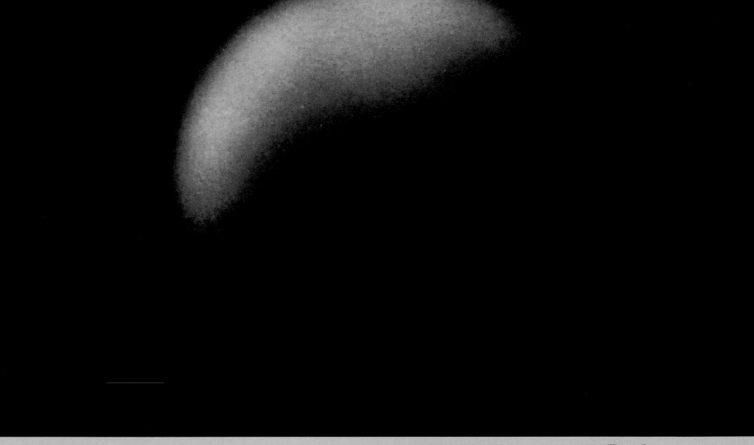

Venus

DISTANCE FROM SUN	67 million miles
ORBITAL PERIOD	225 Earth days
ROTATION PERIOD	243 Earth days
DIAMETER	7,520 miles (95% of Earth's)
MASS	82% of Earth's
TEMPERATURE (surface)	850 °F
MOONS	0

Venus is the brightest object in the night sky. It outshines everything but our Moon and is ten times brighter than the brightest star. Like Mercury, Venus is inside Earth's orbit. Because of this, we always have to look more or less toward the Sun to see it. Venus appears to be the brilliant "morning star" just before sunrise or the glittering "evening star" just after sunset.

Since Venus is our nearest neighbor, you might think that scientists know more about it than any other planet. But it is difficult to study because it is constantly veiled in clouds. Earth is not always cloudy—when the clouds part, astronauts have a spectacular view of the land below. Venus is always cloudy, everywhere. Astronomers looking through the most powerful telescopes cannot see its surface; even spacecraft can photograph only the cloud tops.

Venus looks like a pale yellow, featureless disk. It gives no clue to what lies beneath the clouds. For centuries, scientists had very little information about the planet. Imaginations ran wild. Maybe Venus was a lush tropical jungle; maybe this steamy world was inhabited by intelligent Venusians.

Then, in the late 1950s, observations of radio waves from the planet revealed that the temperature on Venus was a blazing 850 degrees Fahrenheit. Our ideas about the planet changed overnight. There are no lush tropical jungles and certainly no intelligent Venusians. Venus is a furnace.

Scientists expected Venus to be hot because it is near the Sun. They thought it would be a little over 100 degrees Fahrenheit—hotter than all but the hottest days on Earth. They were shocked to find that Venus is much, much hotter than that. It is hotter than Mercury, the

Venus has often been called Earth's "sister planet." It is our nearest planetary neighbor and almost the same size and composition as Earth. When the two planets first formed, they were nearly identical. Now they are about as different as can be. Earth is a living planet. It has a moderate climate, cool ocean breezes, and plants and animals everywhere. Venus is an inferno. Its suffocating carbon dioxide atmosphere creates a greenhouse effect that makes it the hottest planet in the solar system. Its water has long since boiled away. There is nothing alive on Venus.

Venus (far left) in the sky above the Denver Post Office.

closest planet to the Sun; it is hot enough that lead would melt on its surface. Why is our sister planet so unbearably hot?

Venus is hot because it has a very, very thick atmosphere made almost entirely of carbon dioxide. This thick shroud of carbon dioxide creates an enormous greenhouse effect, raising the temperature on the surface an extra 700 degrees Fahrenheit.

When sunlight strikes Venus's atmosphere, much of it is reflected back to space by the high clouds, but the rest makes it to the surface. The sunlight heats the ground. The warm ground tries to cool off by radiating the heat back out toward space as infrared radiation. If this infrared radiation could make it back out through the atmosphere as easily as the sunlight makes it in, there would be no greenhouse effect. But certain gases, such as carbon dioxide, absorb infrared radiation. On Venus, the thick carbon dioxide atmosphere traps the heat before it can escape. The atmosphere acts as a one-way mirror: it lets the sunlight in but doesn't let the infrared radiation back out.

In the early 1960s, scientists began to study Venus using radio waves beamed from large radar antennas on Earth. The radio waves were able to penetrate the clouds and reach the surface. This technique was used, as

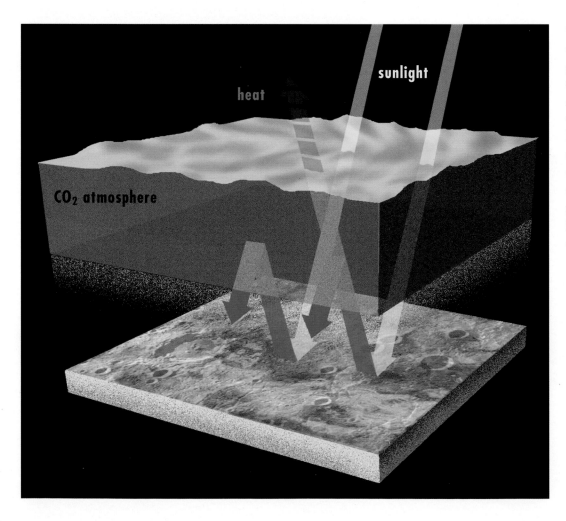

The greenhouse effect. Visible light from the Sun is absorbed by the ground and reradiated as heat. Carbon dioxide, water vapor, and other "greenhouse gases" absorb the heat, trapping the energy and heating the planet. The amount of warming depends on the amount of greenhouse gases in a planet's atmosphere. Venus has a huge greenhouse effect because there is so much carbon dioxide in its atmosphere.

it was on Mercury, to measure the planet's rotation.

Venus rotates on its axis very, very slowly—only once every 243 Earth days. And it rotates "backward." If you looked down on the planet, you would see that instead of spinning in the direction that it orbits the Sun (counter-clockwise), it spins in the opposite direction (clockwise). Scientists believe that Venus suffered a jarring collision early in its history that jolted it into this "retrograde" rotation.

As soon as the Space Age began, Venus became a favorite target for exploration. Twenty-two automated spacecraft have visited the planet since 1962. The early ones simply flew past and sent pictures and data back to Earth. Later, several spacecraft went into orbit around Venus. Even from a close distance, their instruments had trouble seeing through the clouds. Some sent probes screaming into the atmosphere to transmit data back to Earth before they were crushed by the thick air or melted by the intense heat.

Ten spacecraft, all Russian, have actually landed on Venus. The first, *Venera 7*, touched down in 1970; the last, *Vega 2*, in 1985. These amazing machines were a cross between a spacecraft and a deep-ocean diving bell. They survived the pressure that would crush normal spacecraft and the temperatures that would melt most metal. Most were able to send about an hour of data back to Earth before being destroyed by the hostile conditions. In that short time they took the only

When viewed from above, Venus orbits the Sun in a counterclockwise direction. But unlike most planets, it spins in the opposite (clockwise) direction.

A mock-up of the *Venera 13* spacecraft (right) and lander (left) on display at the Cosmos Pavilion in Moscow. The lander rode to Venus inside the large sphere on top of the spacecraft.

closeup pictures, and direct measurements, of the surface of Venus. The landers found that the searing temperature is nearly, but not quite, hot enough to melt the planet's rocks. The surface is so hot that Venus has been baked dry. There is no water anywhere—it boiled away long ago.

Scientists now have a good map of the surface of Venus. It was created from radar data collected by the *Magellan* spacecraft. *Magellan* orbited Venus from 1990 to 1994. It carried a powerful radar that could send signals through the Venusian cloud cover and chart the planet's surface, strip by strip.

The rolling Venusian plains have large vol-

Below left: The *Magellan* spacecraft in the cargo bay of the space shuttle, just before it was sent to Venus. (*Space shuttle*)

Below right: This 3-D view of the surface of Venus was created by combining *Magellan* radar images and topographical data. The two volcanoes are Sif Mons (left) and Gula Mons (right). Lava flows from Sif Mons extend for thousands of miles (center). The vertical scale is exaggerated ten times to show details.

canic craters, deep trenches, high plateaus, and towering mountains. These features are similar in size to those found on Earth. For example, the highest plateau on Venus is about four miles above the plains, like the Tibetan Plateau on Earth; the highest mountains on Venus are over five miles high, like Mount Everest in the Himalayas.

The interior of Venus is still hot and molten. Its surface has been pushed and pulled by forces deep inside the planet, creating folded mountains, fractured plains, and wrinkled land. Molten rock has risen through the crust and spilled onto the surface. The vast rolling plains are layered with baked lava and

dotted with thousands of small volcanoes.

There are much larger volcanoes, too. Huge ones—hundreds of miles across and five miles high—have built up over "hot spots" where lava has punched through the crust in the same place time after time. Many of the volcanoes are probably still active today.

The volcanoes spew gases, such as carbon dioxide and sulfur dioxide, high into the air. The sulfur dioxide combines with water to form sulfuric acid. These toxic droplets form the high clouds that surround Venus and block our view of its surface.

Long, winding rivers of lava stretch for thousands of miles. Some are longer than the

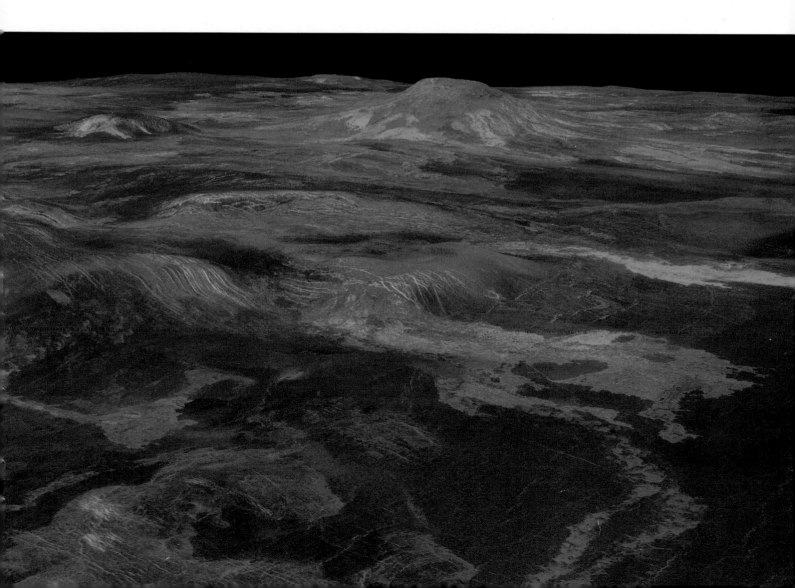

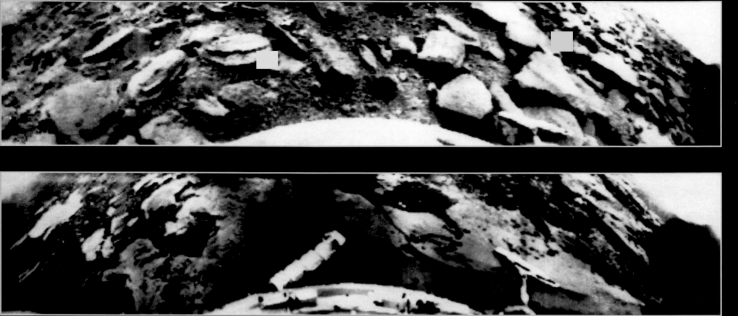

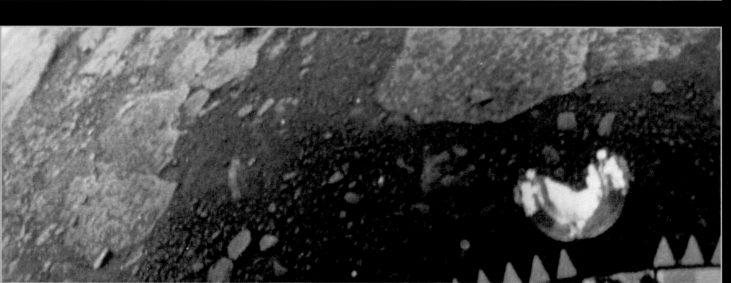

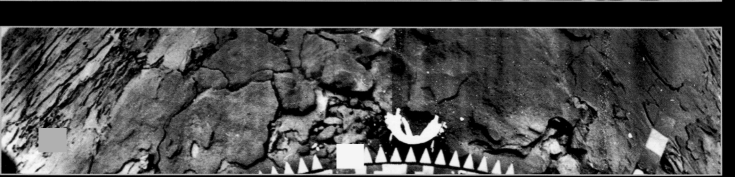

Mississippi River; they cut channels and create deltas, just as rivers of water do on Earth.

In hundreds of places around the planet the ground has been pushed up from below by rising blobs of hot magma. The magma didn't break through the crust but instead created domes of land. The domes later sagged back down and fractured in a series of circular rings. These features, called "coronae," can be as large as 1,500 miles across.

It is difficult to imagine sending astronauts to the surface of this deadly planet. But if astronauts did touch down on Venus, they would never leave the protection of their heavily shielded lander. They would peer out onto an eerie overcast world. They might use

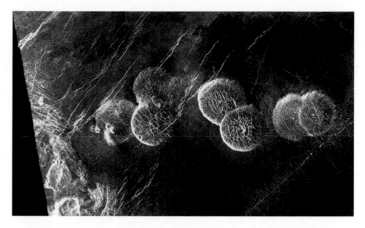

These odd-looking pancake domes are made of lava. Each is about fifteen miles across and two thousand feet high. They formed when molasses-thick lava oozed up through the crust and piled up instead of flowing across the surface. (*Magellan*)

robotic arms to gather samples of rock, and sniffers to analyze samples of air, but they wouldn't risk staying long. They would be happy to be heading home!

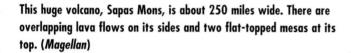

This huge volcano, Sapas Mons, is about 250 miles wide. There are overlapping lava flows on its sides and two flat-topped mesas at its top. (*Magellan*)

The giant circular ring is a 120-mile-wide corona. Pancake domes can be seen around it. (*Magellan*)

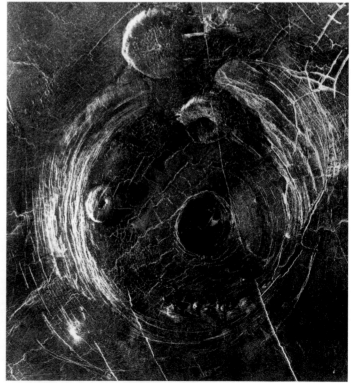

Earth. (*Galileo,* on its way to Jupiter)

Earth

DISTANCE FROM SUN	93 million miles
ORBITAL PERIOD	365.3 days
ROTATION PERIOD	23 hours 56 minutes
DIAMETER	7,926 miles
MASS	5.97×10^{24} kilograms
TEMPERATURE (surface)	-125 to +130 °F
	(mean: 60 °F)
MOONS	1

It is easy to forget that we live on a planet. But if you could step off the surface and look down on Earth from above, you would see that it hurtles around the Sun in the blackness of space and spins on its axis like a top. It takes twenty-four hours for Earth to spin around once. We call that one day. It takes 365 days for Earth to travel around the Sun. We call that one year. Even our measures of time are linked to the motions of our planet.

Like the other terrestrial planets, Earth has a dense iron-rich core, a thick, partially molten mantle surrounding the core, and a thin outer crust. The crust is as thin by comparison as the skin of an apple.

Earth is similar to Mercury, Venus, and Mars in many ways. But it is unique because most of its surface is covered by shimmering blue oceans.

When Earth first formed, water could not

exist on its seething sea of molten rock. As the planet began to cool, its rocky crust solidified. Steam and other hot gases escaped into the early atmosphere through volcanic vents and cracks in the crust. The water vapor in the air condensed into clouds, then poured down as rain. Soon, oceans of water filled Earth's low basins.

If you could look back in time four billion years, you would not recognize the planet you live on. The young Earth was a noisy, dangerous place. Bolts of lightning crackled in stormy skies; sheets of rain drenched barren lands; red-hot lava oozed through cracks in the crust; and fiery meteors crushed the ground. Yet in the midst of all this, something extraordinary was happening: life was beginning.

There are only three basic ingredients

Earth, like Mercury and Venus, is basically a ball of rock in orbit around a star. But our home planet is very different from every other. Its vast blue oceans make it a special world. No other place in the solar system has even a drop of water on its surface. With water, Earth became a living planet. Its sister, Venus, also has mountains, valleys, and deserts. But green forests climb Earth's mountains, rivers wind through its valleys, and even its deserts are alive with plants and animals. Our planet is an oasis in space.

Artist's cutaway painting of Earth. Earth's solid core is surrounded by a partially molten mantle and a thin, rocky crust.

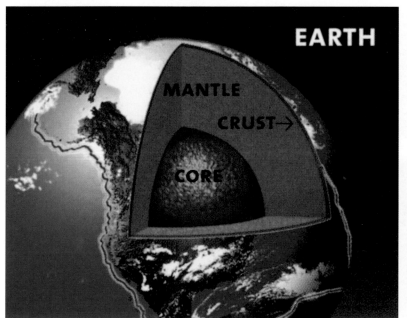

Satellites are used to observe and study Earth. This shows the temperature of Earth's oceans. The coolest water is in blue and purple; the warmest water is in red and white. (*TOPEX/Poseidon*)

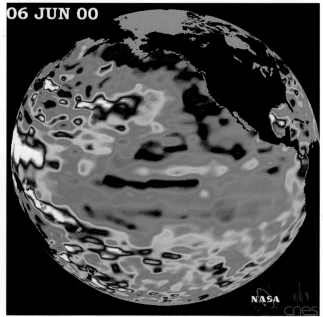

necessary for life: water, organic molecules, and an energy source. All these were available on early Earth.

Water is vital for life. Life started in water and, to this day, all living things need it to survive. Water makes up two-thirds of every living thing, from a single-celled microbe to a many-celled mouse. The watery environment inside cells allows the chemical reactions that keep organisms alive to occur.

The elements carbon, hydrogen, oxygen, and nitrogen are also essential for life. These are among the most common elements in the solar system. They were present on Earth when it formed and were continuously deliv-

Space shuttle astronauts took this picture of one of Earth's vast oceans. The tail of the shuttle is visible near the top of the photo.

To a person standing on Earth, it looks as if the Sun moves across our sky. But it is our planet that is moving. Earth spins around once every twenty-four hours; any given location rotates into the sunlight at dawn and out of the sunlight at dusk.

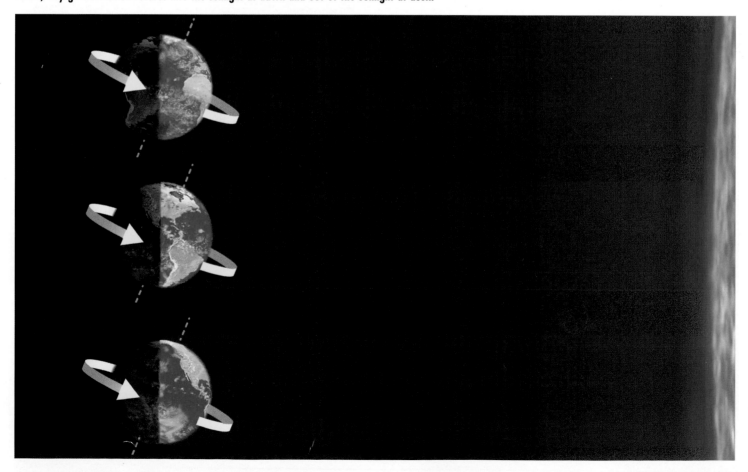

ered to the planet by the planetesimals that bombarded its surface. Simple molecules made of combinations of these elements circulated in the early oceans.

The oceans provided a place for molecules—some drained from the land and some washed from the atmosphere—to collect and mix. Then some form of energy—perhaps heat from the Sun, lightning from the sky, or steam from inside the planet—combined these simple molecules into more complex organic molecules, the molecules that make up living things.

In just a few hundred million years, the first living organisms formed out of the brew of organic molecules in the waters of early Earth. These primitive, tiny living things were able to make copies of themselves from the organic molecules in their environment. But this process was not always perfect. By chance, some organisms were better able to compete for the organic molecules than others. Evolution had begun.

No one knows for certain where this process started. Life may have begun in shallow tide pools warmed by sunlight, where daily tides delivered a fresh supply of organic molecules. It may have begun in undersea volcanic vents, where molten magma boiled the waters and enriched them with nutrients.

Earth orbits the Sun in one year. During that time, the seasons change because Earth's axis of rotation is tilted (by 23.5 degrees). During part of the orbit, the Northern Hemisphere is tilted toward the Sun (lower left) and sunlight shines more directly on this half of the planet. It is summer in the north and winter in the south. Six months later, the Sun shines most directly on the southern half of the planet (lower right), so it's summer south of the equator.

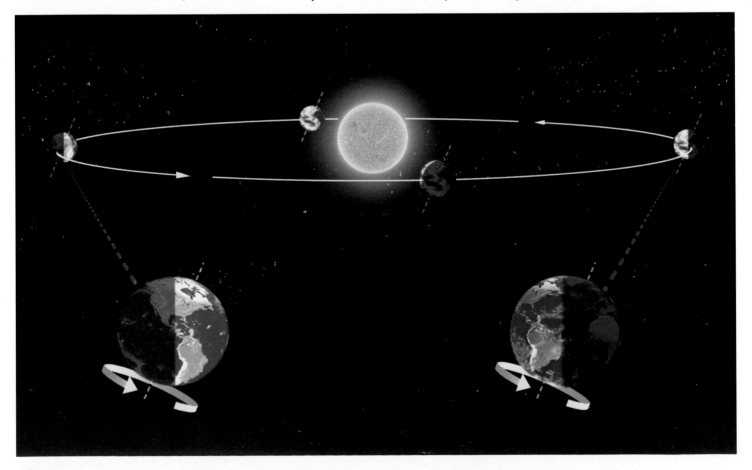

The earliest forms of recognizable life were tiny single cells that looked like today's bacteria. For nearly three billion years—most of our planet's history—microscopic organisms like these were the only life on Earth.

At first, they were very primitive. But slowly some evolved new ways to get food from their environment. Eventually, their microscopic descendants were able to use the energy in sunlight and carbon dioxide in the atmosphere to make their own food. As part of this process, called "photosynthesis," oxygen was released. One by one, millennium after millennium, oxygen molecules bubbled out of the waters and collected in the air.

By about 800 million years ago, more complex forms of life had evolved in the oceans. Green algae floated in sunlit waters, and the first soft-bodied animals left their tracks and burrows on the ocean floor.

About 400 million years ago, corals built reefs around islands, jellyfish glided on ocean currents, and starfish crowded the seas. At about this same time, green plants began to colonize the continents. Plants also perform photosynthesis and add oxygen to the air. The

Artist's painting of Earth as it might have looked about four billion years ago. Primitive life appeared shortly after the oceans formed.

Fossils of primitive microscopic organisms found in rocks from western Australia show that life existed on our planet as early as 3.5 billion years ago. Chains of these tiny organisms look like certain bacteria that live in the oceans today.

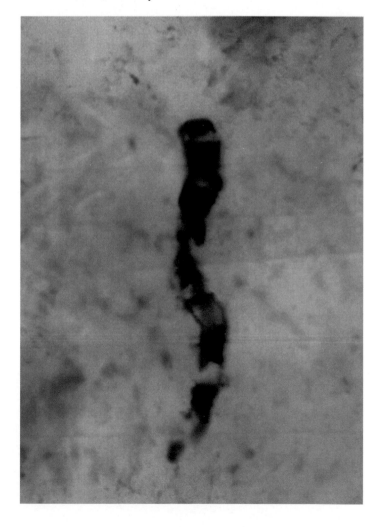

first plants were very small and could grow only where it was very wet. Later, they evolved roots that let them drink water stored underground; some developed clever ways to conserve water that let them grow in even the driest places. Once plants began to spread across the valleys, mountains, and deserts, other living things were able to follow. Plants provided food and shelter for other forms of life.

By 100 million years ago, fish swam in the oceans; birds flew in the skies; small mammals scurried over the lands; and insects were everywhere. But dinosaurs were the dominant

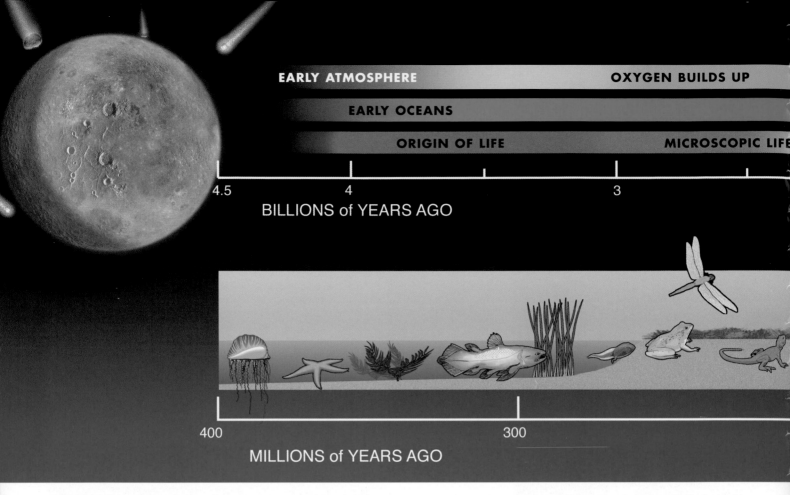

EARLY ATMOSPHERE   OXYGEN BUILDS UP

EARLY OCEANS

ORIGIN OF LIFE   MICROSCOPIC LIFE

4.5   4   3

BILLIONS of YEARS AGO

400   300

MILLIONS of YEARS AGO

Earth timeline 4.5 billion years ago to the present, showing the approximate times of some important stages of our planet's evolution. The lower scale shows only the last 400 million years of Earth's long history. Human beings are very recent newcomers, occupying less than the last 1/100 of an inch of the lower scale.

creatures of this time. Plant-eaters walked the valleys, and meat-eaters struck fear in the hearts of other animals. The dinosaurs left their footprints and fossils all over the world.

Our planet has supported life for a very long time. In that time, countless species have come and gone. About sixty-five million years ago, the dinosaurs and many other kinds of animals and plants disappeared. This mass extinction was probably caused by a giant asteroid or comet that struck the Earth. Such mass extinctions have happened many times since life evolved, but each time some species survived.

By about ten million years ago, the ancestors of modern cats, dogs, birds, fish, and insects lived on our planet. Human beings were still nowhere to be found. We have inhabited Earth for only a few hundred thousand years—just the last instant of our planet's long history.

Today, a life-sustaining atmosphere surrounds our planet; four oceans cover nearly three-fourths of its surface; seven continents cover the rest. Living things are everywhere.

From the moment that our planet's atmosphere, land, and oceans formed, they were linked together by cycles that move air, rock,

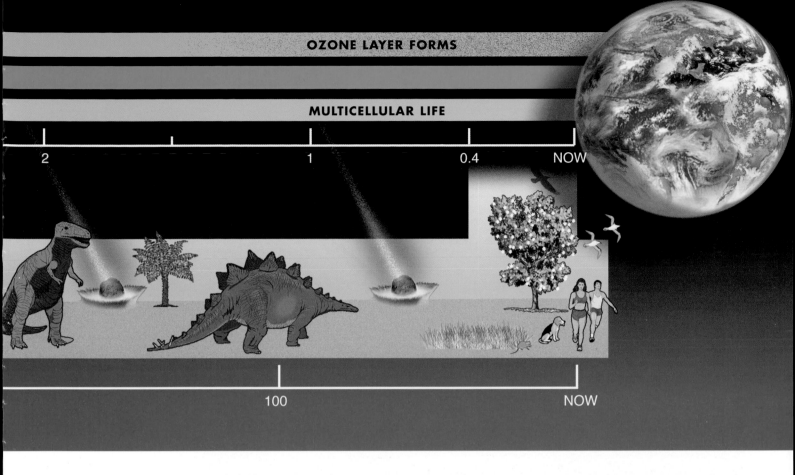

OZONE LAYER FORMS

MULTICELLULAR LIFE

2 1 0.4 NOW

100 NOW

Very few of Earth's impact craters are still visible. This photograph shows the Manicouagan crater near Quebec, Canada. It was formed about 200 million years ago and is now heavily eroded. The crater is almost forty-five miles across. (*Space shuttle*)

Space shuttle astronauts took this photograph of Earth's atmosphere at sunrise. The storm clouds rise almost ten miles high.

and water from place to place. Once life evolved, it became a part of these cycles, too. Winds in the atmosphere drive ocean currents; water evaporates from the oceans and returns as rain over the lands; oxygen is given off by plants and taken in by animals; and volcanoes throw tons of gas into the air from deep inside the Earth. These natural cycles connect the atmosphere, oceans, lands, and living things and maintain our planet's livable conditions.

Earth's atmosphere is a thin blanket of air that insulates our planet from the extreme con-

ditions of space. It helps to keep the planet warm and protects us from the Sun's ultraviolet radiation.

Today, our air is made mostly of nitrogen and oxygen gases. It includes very small amounts of such other molecules as water vapor, carbon dioxide, and ozone. Although this composition seems normal to us, it is strikingly different from the atmospheres of the other terrestrial planets. The air on Venus is almost entirely carbon dioxide; so is the air on Mars. Neither contains any oxygen.

In fact, you would not expect to find oxygen in a planet's atmosphere since it is one of the most reactive gases in the solar system. On Venus and Mars, nearly all the oxygen reacted with other molecules to form more stable compounds. This happened on our planet, too. But once life on Earth evolved, it began to add fresh oxygen to our air. There is oxygen in our atmosphere because there is life on our planet.

Although there are only traces of water vapor and carbon dioxide in Earth's atmosphere, these gases are vital to our climate. Both are "greenhouse gases"—they absorb heat that our planet radiates back toward space and trap it in the atmosphere. There is only a modest greenhouse effect on Earth— nothing like the suffocating greenhouse on

Venus—but it is enough to warm our planet's surface by nearly 60 degrees Fahrenheit. Earth would be a frozen wasteland without it.

Oceans cover about 75% of our planet's surface. Ocean currents, driven by the Earth's rotation, move rivers of salt water around the world. The currents slowly stir the waters, carrying nutrients from one place to another and moving heat from the equator to the poles.

As the Sun heats the surface of the ocean, water molecules evaporate and drift up into the sky. When they reach cooler air, they condense into tiny droplets that form clouds. Winds blow the clouds over the land, and the water falls to Earth as rain. Rain falls on mountains and valleys, bringing water to plants and animals that depend on it for their

The atmospheres of Venus and Mars are mostly carbon dioxide. Earth's atmosphere is very different. It is almost 80% nitrogen and over 20% oxygen.

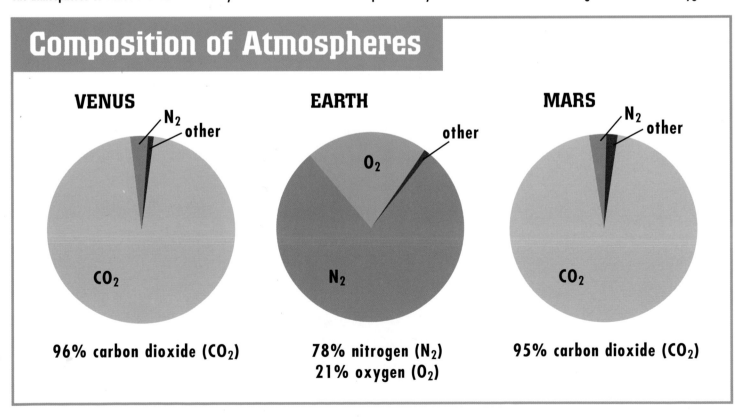

Composition of Atmospheres

VENUS
N_2 other
CO_2
96% carbon dioxide (CO_2)

EARTH
other
O_2
N_2
78% nitrogen (N_2)
21% oxygen (O_2)

MARS
N_2 other
CO_2
95% carbon dioxide (CO_2)

Looking down on Mount Everest (center) in the Himalaya Mountains. The mountains were formed when the tectonic plate carrying India collided into Asia. The land was crumpled and lifted, creating the world's tallest mountains. Today, the plate carrying India is still moving about two inches each year, and the Himalayas are still growing about a tenth of an inch each year. (*Space shuttle*)

survival. Streams flow downhill and merge into rivers that carry water back to the ocean. This cycle delivers fresh water around the world.

Earth is an active planet. Its surface is continually being reshaped and relayered by forces from deep within. On Earth, as on Venus, molten rock below the surface drives the change. But while Venus's crust is apparently one thick shell, Earth's thinner crust is broken into several enormous pieces called "plates." The plates float like rocky rafts on the molten mantle, carrying continents with them as they inch across the planet.

The continents stand high above the oceans because their crust is thicker and lighter than the crust of the ocean basins. The thinner ocean crust has long cracks that extend thousands of miles along the ocean floor. Earth's plates are driven by molten magma that rises through these cracks. When the magma hits the cold ocean water, it cools and forms new crust. The new crust pushes apart old crust and drives the plates. The motion of the plates, called "plate tectonics," doesn't happen on any other planet.

Although it is not obvious in a human lifetime, our planet is always changing.

Continents sail across its surface; mountains are pushed skyward, then erode and disappear; asteroids crash into the planet, changing the climate and killing entire species. But through it all Earth has sustained life. It has remained habitable for billions of years because of the exquisite cycles that connect its air, land, water, and life.

Human beings have existed for only a short span of time. Yet in that time, we have become an important force on our planet. City lights outline the continents; paved highways crisscross the land; and massive dams control the flow of rivers. Our challenge for the future is to avoid disrupting Earth's natural cycles while we continue to advance our civilization.

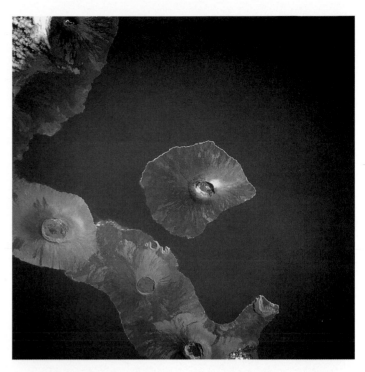

The Galápagos Islands are a chain of volcanic islands off the coast of South America. They are located on a volcanic "hot spot," where plumes of hot magma rise up through the crust to form an underwater volcano, which may grow tall enough to become an island. Because its tectonic plate is constantly moving, the island eventually moves past the hot spot, making room for another island to form. Isla Fernandina (center) is one of the most active volcanoes in the world. (*Space shuttle*)

Earth at night. This is a composite of hundreds of photographs taken by orbiting satellites. City lights illuminate the continents. In some parts of the world — such as the eastern United States, Europe, India, and Japan — the lights of the cities blend together. Some parts of the planet are sparsely populated. The deserts and rain forests are dark; so are Greenland, the Arctic, and Antarctica.

The Moon

The Moon.

DISTANCE FROM EARTH	239,000 miles
ORBITAL PERIOD (around Earth)	27.3 days
ROTATION PERIOD	27.3 days
DIAMETER	2,159 miles (27% of Earth's)
MASS	1.2% of Earth's
TEMPERATURE	-272 to +243 °F

The Moon is our constant companion. It is much closer than any of the planets, circling our world as we orbit the Sun. Its distinct light and dark markings are visible to the naked eye. The Moon has practically no atmosphere and its ancient surface is covered with craters. Temperatures change dramatically from day to night. When the Sun is high in the sky, temperatures peak at nearly 250 degrees Fahrenheit. But during the long lunar night, temperatures plunge to 270 degrees below zero. The Moon is as far from Earth as astronauts have ever traveled.

Earth is the only terrestrial planet with a large moon. Mercury has no moon. Neither does Venus. Mars has two tiny moons, each only a few miles across. Our Moon is huge by comparison—it is nearly as big as Mercury!

Our planet has not always had a moon. In the early days of the solar system, the young, moonless Earth was smashed by an object about the size of Mars. The catastrophic collision turned Earth's surface into liquid and splattered a huge blob of vaporized rock into space. The blob went into orbit around our planet and eventually came together to form the Moon.

As the Moon cooled, a solid crust formed and became the lunar highlands. The highlands were soon dimpled with craters of all sizes. Some of the craters filled with lava that oozed up through the crust and became the lunar *maria*, or seas.

Even without a telescope, it's easy to see the light-colored highlands and the dark-

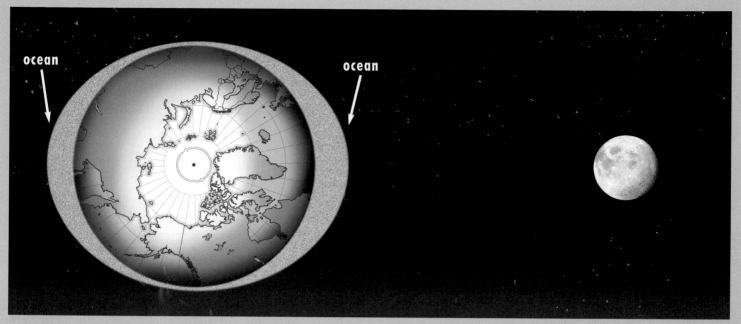

ocean

ocean

An artist's exaggerated drawing, looking down on Earth, shows how the gravitational pull between the Moon and the Earth causes Earth's tides. High tides occur on both the side of Earth closest to the Moon and the side farthest from the Moon. The side nearest the Moon feels the strongest pull, the intermediate sides of the Earth a weaker pull, and the side farthest from the Moon the weakest pull. As a result, the water in the oceans nearest the Moon gets pulled toward the Moon, and the water in the oceans farthest from the Moon gets "left behind." The result is high tides on both sides of the Earth. Since the Earth is rotating, that means that a beach on Earth sees two high tides a day — one when it is nearest the Moon, and one when it is farthest away.

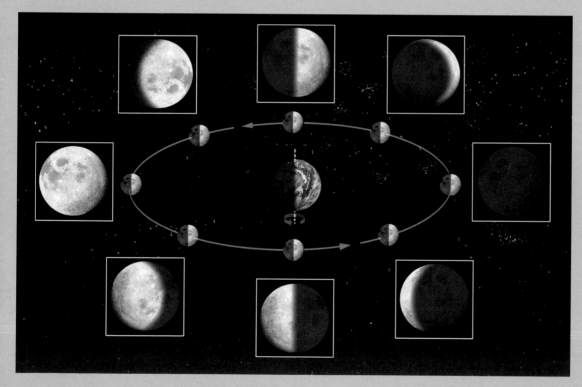

The phase of the Moon (how much of it appears illuminated) depends on the geometrical relationships between the Earth, the Sun, and the location of the Moon in its orbit. The boxes show the Moon as it would appear to a person standing on Earth.

colored maria. The highlands stand thousands of feet above the maria and are heavily cratered. The maria are round, smooth plains of frozen lava with relatively few craters.

Today, the Moon is a dead world. It has no air, no water, and no internal activity. This means that there is no wind or rain to erode the land and there are no volcanic eruptions

Astronaut John Young puts away his tools and gets ready to drive the lunar rover back to the lunar lander. (*Apollo 16*)

The tracks of a lunar rover are still etched in the Moon's soil. (*Apollo 14*)

to repave the surface. The ancient lunar landscape is frozen in time. The oldest rocks from the highlands are 4.4 billion years old, nearly as old as the solar system itself. Even the lava of the relatively young maria dates back 3.2 to 3.9 billion years.

The Earth and the Moon are bound together by gravity. As the Earth tugs on the Moon, it slowly changes the Moon's rotation and orbit. As the Moon tugs on Earth, it slightly changes the planet's rotation. This is slowly synchronizing the motions of the Earth and Moon.

Four billion years ago, the Moon was much closer to the Earth than it is today. Since then it has gradually been creeping away from us. It is still moving about one and a half inches farther away each year. Meanwhile, the Moon's rotation has slowed down. It now rotates once every twenty-seven days and eight hours—exactly the same time that it takes the Moon to circle the Earth. As a result, when the Moon orbits Earth, the same side is facing us all the time.

On a historic day in July 1969, astronaut Neil Armstrong became the first person to set foot on another world. His bulky spacesuit kept him alive and allowed him to step outside onto the lunar surface, even though there was no air to breathe and no atmosphere to protect him from the Sun's radiation. The spacesuit was very heavy on Earth—but not on the Moon. The gravity on the surface of the Moon is only one-sixth the gravity that holds us to the surface of Earth, so everything on the Moon weighs one-sixth what it does on Earth. Neil Armstrong weighed only about thirty pounds!

Between 1969 and 1972, six U.S. space missions landed twelve astronauts on the Moon. These explorers from Earth rambled across the maria, chipped at lunar rocks, and bounded up crater rims. The 2,200 moon rocks they carried back to Earth have helped scientists to piece together the story of the Moon's origin and the age of the solar system.

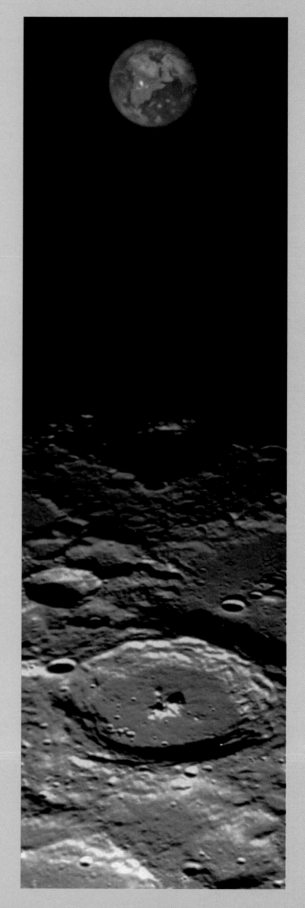

The Moon's surface, with Earth visible in the night sky. (Clementine)

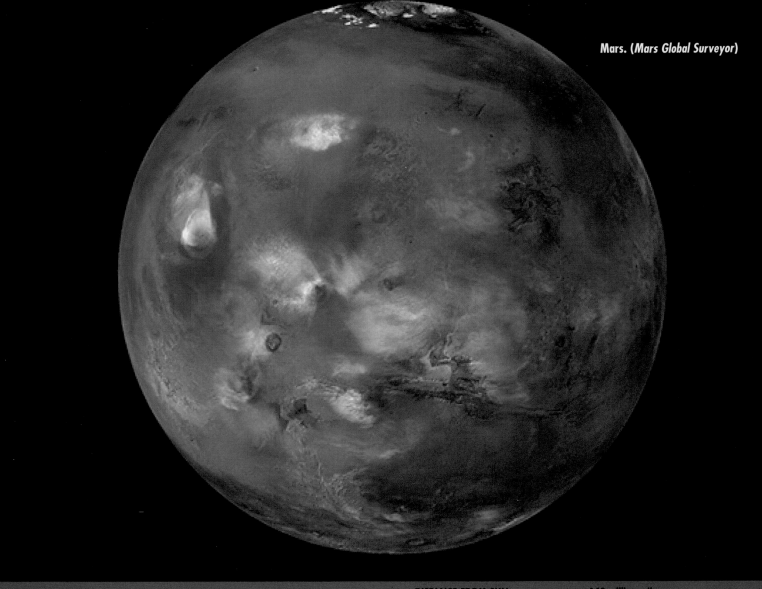

Mars

DISTANCE FROM SUN	142 million miles
ORBITAL PERIOD	1.9 Earth years
ROTATION PERIOD	24.6 hours
DIAMETER	4,217 miles (53% of Earth's)
MASS	11% of Earth's
TEMPERATURE (surface)	-190 to +60 °F
	(mean: -70 °F)
MOONS	2

This bright reddish point of light has intrigued stargazers for centuries. Generations of astronomers, poets, and writers wondered whether Mars was like Earth. They wondered whether there were intelligent Martians curious about the bluish point of light visible in their sky and about the earthlings who might inhabit it.

Mars is easier to study from Earth than Mercury or Venus. The planet is often high in the night sky, and Earth-based telescopes can see to its surface.

Astronomers have long known that it takes Mars almost two Earth years—nearly twice as long as Earth—to travel once around the Sun. And even blurry views through early telescopes revealed that Mars, like Earth, spins like a top. It rotates on its axis once every

50

twenty-four hours and thirty-seven minutes. A day on Mars is just a little longer than a day on Earth. An astronaut on Mars would see the Sun rise in the east, travel across the sky for about twelve hours, and set in the west, just as on Earth.

But even the best Earth-based telescopes had a fuzzy view of Mars. The planet came into sharper focus in 1965, when the *Mariner 4* spacecraft flew past and sent back the first closeup photographs of the planet. Several other spacecraft followed. Some circled Mars for years and sent back detailed pictures of the planet below. Three landers—*Viking 1, Viking 2,* and *Pathfinder*—touched down on the surface. They found Mars to be a much more pleasant planet than Venus. These spacecraft were able to operate on Mars for months

Mars, *the fourth planet from the Sun, is smaller and lighter than Earth. It is a red, rugged world, with volcanoes poking through thin clouds and sheer cliffs disappearing into deep canyons. Today, the planet is cold, dry, and desolate. There is no water on its surface, no oxygen in its air, and no life in its soil. But there is evidence that ancient Mars was very different. Billions of years ago, Mars may have been a warmer planet — perhaps with ice-covered lakes, a shallow sea, and possibly even primitive microscopic life.*

Sojourner was the first rover to explore the surface of Mars. About the size of a small dog, it was carried to Mars by the *Pathfinder* spacecraft in 1997. (*Pathfinder*)

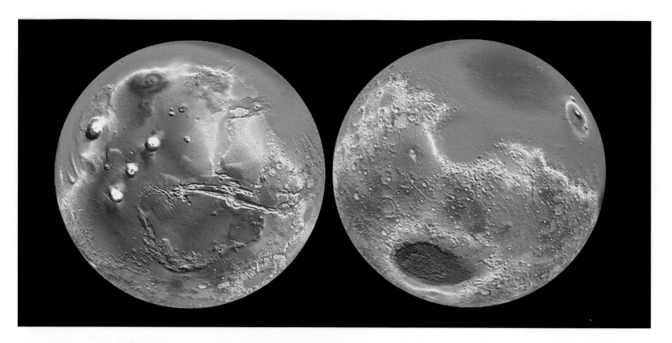

False-color map showing the topography of Mars. The highest elevations are in red and white, the lowest in blue and purple. (Left) The raised Tharsis region, with four towering volcanoes, shown in white (including Olympus Mons, farthest left). (Right) The southern part of Mars is higher than the northern part and has more craters. The Hellas Basin, an impact crater 1,300 miles across and six miles deep, is visible at the bottom, in purple. (*Mars Global Surveyor*)

or years—much, much longer than those that touched down on Venus. Through the eyes of the landers we could gaze out onto the red dust and gray rocks of the Martian plains.

Mars is a cold, windswept planet. Its atmosphere is thin and its red surface is bone-dry. But its history is fascinating. Huge volcanoes that formed on a younger, more active Mars dwarf the highest mountains on Earth. Dry riverbeds hint that water flowed across the ancient Martian highlands four billion years ago. Ultra-smooth plains, the flattest land in the solar system, may once have been covered by a huge ocean of water.

The northern and southern hemispheres of Mars almost seem to belong to two different planets. The land in the south has changed very little over nearly four billion years. These Martian highlands are covered with craters and etched with ancient riverbeds. The land in the north is about three miles lower than the land in the south and is very smooth. Part of it has been paved over by lava, and part may once have been covered by a shallow ocean.

Though much of Mars's surface hasn't changed for billions of years, some of it has been pushed and stretched by forces underground. When Mars was young, it was very hot inside. Like Venus and Earth, its hot interior churned. A broad area of land was pushed up by molten rock and now swells six miles above the rest of the planet. This vast region is called the Tharsis Bulge.

The Tharsis region is home to hundreds of volcanoes. Enormous volcanic peaks pierce the high Martian clouds. The mountains on

Earth and the volcanoes on Venus are tiny by comparison.

Olympus Mons, the largest mountain in the solar system, rises just off the western edge of the Tharsis region. This magnificent volcano is more than sixteen miles high—three times higher than the tallest mountain on Earth.

Because Mars is smaller than Earth and Venus, it cooled more quickly. It is possible that a few Martian volcanoes are still active, but no eruptions have ever been seen. Most occurred billions of years ago, when Mars was still a young planet.

The bulging Tharsis region has split and cracked, creating networks of deep canyons—huge fractures in the planet's crust that stretch for thousands of miles. Valles Marineris is the longest and the deepest canyon in the solar system. It would stretch all the way across the United States and would swallow the Grand

Olympus Mons, the highest mountain in the solar system, rises above the Martian clouds. (*Mariner 9*)

Valles Marineris. This great canyon would stretch across the United States. (*Viking*)

The *Viking 2* lander's robot arm scoops up a sample of Martian soil and leaves its mark in the ground. (*Viking 2*)

Canyon without a trace. If an astronaut kicked a rock off the rim of Valles Marineris, it could tumble four miles before hitting the canyon floor.

The atmosphere of Mars, like that of Venus, is made mostly of carbon dioxide. But Mars's atmosphere is very, very thin. The Martian air is almost 100 times thinner than the air on Earth and 10,000 times thinner than the air on Venus. There are crystals of ice in the wispy Martian clouds, but the air is too thin and too cold for raindrops to form.

The farther a planet is from the Sun, the less sunlight strikes its surface. Mars basks in less sunshine than Earth, and its thin atmosphere doesn't provide much of a greenhouse effect. The average temperature on Mars is a frigid 70 degrees below zero Fahrenheit.

Earth's atmosphere acts as a blanket and helps keep our planet warm overnight. But Mars's heat escapes to space as soon as the Sun sets.

During some parts of the year, ferocious Martian winds stir up huge dust storms in the southern hemisphere that sweep across the planet. Fine red dust is suspended in the air and creates a pink Martian sky throughout the year.

This dry, dusty world does not look very hospitable. The *Viking* landers performed experiments to look for signs of life in the Martian soil. Their metal arms scooped up samples of red dirt and carried them inside the landers for analysis. They did not find evidence of life.

It is unlikely that there is life on the surface

of Mars today. The rough landscape is absolutely dry and is bombarded by damaging ultraviolet light from the Sun. But it is possible that primitive life exists beneath the Martian surface, or that life existed on the planet long ago.

Four billion years ago, the ingredients essential for life were present on Mars. Water flowed in the Martian highlands and lapped the shores of a shallow, northern sea. Icy comets carried carbon, hydrogen, nitrogen, and oxygen to the planet. Lava erupting through volcanoes, water boiling near underwater volcanic vents, or lightning crackling in the skies could have provided the necessary spark of energy. Could life have blossomed on this alien world?

It is possible that life started on Mars at about the same time, and in much the same way, that it started on Earth. Life may have

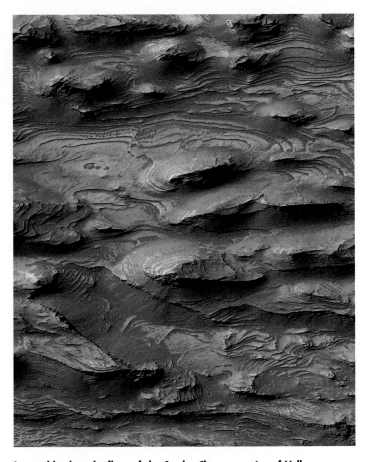

Layered land on the floor of the Candor Chasma portion of Valles Marineris. Patterns like this on Earth are usually the result of sedimentation in a watery environment. Though there are other possible explanations, this could be material that was deposited in a lake or shallow sea. (*Mars Global Surveyor*)

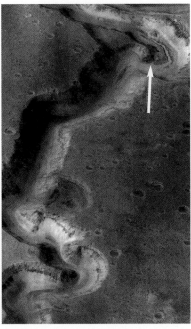

Both *Viking* (left) and *Mars Global Surveyor* (right) photographed this Martian valley cutting through a region in the cratered southern highlands. *Global Surveyor*'s higher-resolution view was the first to show a small inner channel (at the top of the photo). This inner channel suggests that a steady flow of water may have cut the valley.

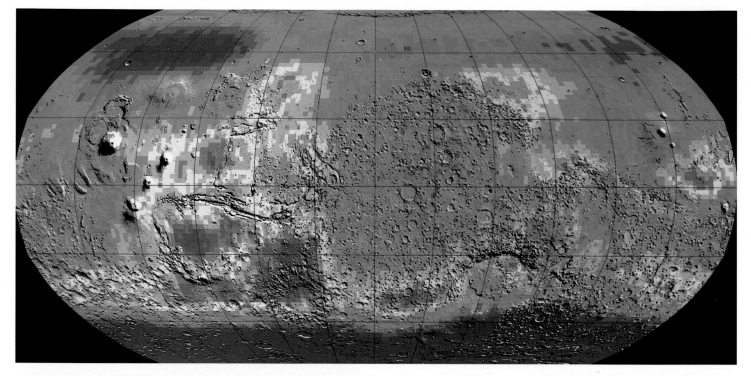

This false-color image shows the distribution of hydrogen (most of it in the form of water ice) within three feet of the Martian surface. The blues indicate areas of highest concentration. Near the south pole, there is enough water ice to fill Lake Michigan several times. Deep blue areas are ice mixed with soil; light blue patches are where water has reacted with rock. (*Mars Odyssey*)

The wall of the Gorgonum Crater has deep channels that may have been carved relatively recently by water flowing through porous rock. (*Mars Global Surveyor*)

started at the bottom of a muddy Martian lake. Or it may have started in volcanic hot springs, like those in Earth's Arctic, where steaming waters rise through the frozen ground.

But conditions on Mars soon began to change. About 3.7 billion years ago, its atmosphere began to thin and its temperature began to drop. Its water slowly disappeared from the surface.

In only a few hundred million years, the icy lakes, water-filled canyons, and muddy red rivers were gone. Mars evolved into a cold, dry planet with a thin carbon dioxide atmosphere and a barren, windswept surface.

If Martian microbes did exist, it is possible they survived by following the water underground. There was still plenty of water

The Sylvan Springs hot springs in Yellowstone National Park, Wyoming.

beneath the surface. It may have been stored in huge reservoirs capped by a thick layer of ice, or in porous underground rocks that soak up water like a sponge.

Microscopic organisms are very hardy. On Earth, they thrive in some of the most unlikely places. Bacteria live in sandstone rock in the frozen deserts of Antarctica, in the boiling hot waters of the Sylvan Springs in Yellowstone National Park, and in solid rock miles underground. Martian microbes might have survived in similar environments—and they might still be there today. Over the next decade, the rovers we send to the surface of Mars will search for signs of underground water and hunt for evidence of microscopic Martian life.

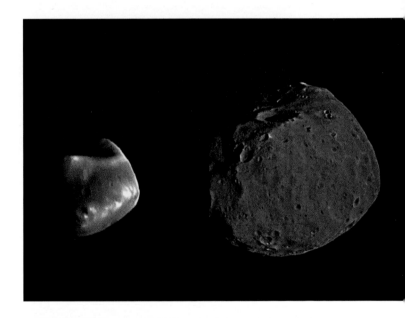

Mars's two small, rocky moons, Deimos (left) and Phobos (right), orbit close to the planet. They are probably asteroids, or maybe pieces of the same asteroid, that were captured by the planet long ago. Deimos is about ten miles wide; Phobos is about seventeen miles wide. (*Viking*)

A sunset on Mars. (*Pathfinder*)

No human has ever set foot on another planet. Mars will be the first that astronauts visit, but not until at least 2015. When they do arrive, they will find a world more like Earth than any other place in the solar system.

As they drive across the rocky terrain, their rover will leave its tracks in the dusty red soil. They will need spacesuits to protect them from the thin Martian air and the extreme cold. The astronauts will chisel on rocks and dig in the ground, looking for evidence of past or present life. Fine red dust will cling to their boots and gloves. When they stop to rest they will look up at a dimmer Sun through a rosy sky loaded with red dust. And at night they will see two tiny moons in the Martian sky.

The world they explore will seem strangely familiar. But there will be no water trickling through the canyons and no grass growing on the mountainsides. Everywhere they look they will see a red planet, a planet without the familiar blues and greens of Earth.

The Asteroid Belt

Asteroids are hunks of rock in orbit around the Sun. They are found many places in the inner solar system, but most are between the orbits of Mars and Jupiter in a region known as the Asteroid Belt.

Astronomers think that asteroids are ancient rocks that never managed to accumulate into a planet. They are fragments of planetesimals—debris left over from the earliest days of the solar system.

Most asteroids are too small to be seen through a telescope. Astronomers have cataloged over 10,000 of them but think that hundreds of thousands more are undiscovered. Ceres, the largest, is 588 miles across. Only two dozen or so are more than 125 miles wide; all the rest are much smaller.

We got our first closeup look at an asteroid in the early 1990s when the *Galileo* spacecraft passed through the Asteroid Belt on its way to Jupiter. It photographed a potato-shaped asteroid named Ida. The old rock is pitted with craters and covered with dust. And much to the surprise of scientists, the photos showed a tiny moon in orbit around the asteroid. In 2001, the *NEAR* spacecraft actually landed on an asteroid. It mapped the twenty-one-mile-long asteroid Eros for a year before touching down on its rocky surface.

Most asteroids don't cross Earth's orbit. But some do. Only very rarely does one of them collide with Earth. But over our planet's long history, many such collisions have occurred. Most of the craters from those impacts have been erased, but about 150 still scar the Earth.

Top: Ida and its moon, Dactyl. Ida is thirty-five miles long; Dactyl is only one mile across. (*Galileo,* on its way to Jupiter)

Left: Most asteroids are found between Mars and Jupiter.

Venus, Earth, and Mars—
Why Are They So Different?

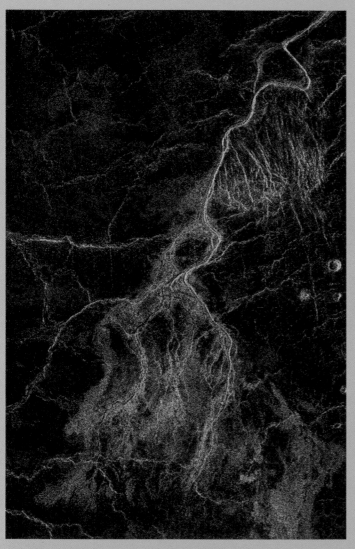

A river of lava forms a river delta on Venus. (*Magellan*)

Venus, Earth, and Mars are vastly different worlds. But four billion years ago, they were very much alike—and very different from the three planets we know today.

Why did these worlds evolve so differently? One reason is that they are different distances from the Sun, but that is not the only reason. Their sizes are also important. Both the size of the planet and the amount of sunlight striking its surface affect the cycling of carbon dioxide between the atmosphere and land. That, in turn, affects the planet's climate.

What happened to the carbon dioxide that made up much of the early atmospheres of the three planets? On Earth, torrential rains carried it from the air down to the ground. Some dissolved in the oceans and some weathered the land, becoming bound in carbonate rock. Some was returned to the air by erupting volcanoes. Carbon dioxide is continually cycled between the land and the air, but most is now stored in Earth's land and oceans, with an important bit left in the atmosphere. If all our carbon dioxide were released into the air, we would have an atmosphere like Venus's, and a greenhouse effect to match!

On Mars, carbon dioxide rained or

The Nile River Delta on Earth. (*Space shuttle*)

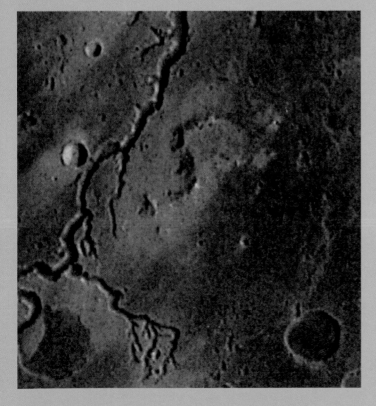

An ancient channel in the southern highlands of Mars. (*Viking*)

snowed out of the atmosphere, too. While the planet still had active volcanoes, it was able to return some to the atmosphere. But Mars is smaller than Earth, so its insides cooled more quickly. One by one, its volcanoes fell silent; less and less carbon dioxide was spewed back into the atmosphere—most remained locked in the land. As Mars's atmosphere thinned, more heat escaped to space. Eventually, its air became very thin, and its temperature very cold. All of the water vanished from its surface.

Venus is closer to the Sun than Earth, so it started out a bit warmer. The temperature difference was small but critical. Much of its water remained in the warmer air—and extended higher into the atmosphere. The Sun's ultraviolet light broke apart the water molecules at the top of the atmosphere, and the atoms escaped to space. Though rain may have been falling, carrying carbon dioxide to

Landscapes of Venus (left), Earth (center), and Mars (right).

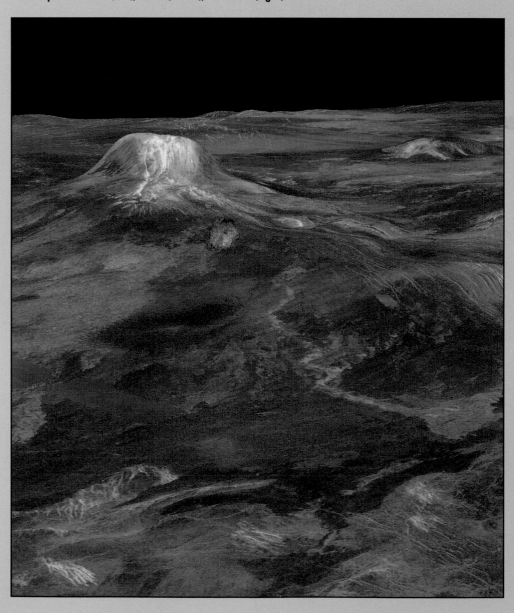

the land, water was also continually being lost to space. Within a few hundred million years, most of the planet's water was gone.

Once the rain stopped, carbon dioxide was no longer removed from the atmosphere of Venus. But it was still being pumped into the air by thousands of active volcanoes. As the carbon dioxide atmosphere got thicker and thicker, an enormous greenhouse developed that baked the planet.

For four billion years, Earth's temperature never got so cold that all its water froze or so hot that its oceans evaporated. It kept its moderate climate and its water. But Venus evolved into a hot, dry inferno; Mars into a cold, arid wasteland. If Earth had been closer to the Sun, it might have ended up like Venus. If Mars had been bigger — say, a little larger than Earth — it might still have a substantial atmosphere and a reasonable climate.

The Giant Planets

The next four planets from the Sun are known as the giant planets. Unlike the rocky inner planets, Jupiter, Saturn, Uranus, and Neptune are much larger, made of light material, and do not have solid surfaces.

The outer layers of each giant are made of gas, which becomes thicker and thicker until it becomes liquid or slush deep inside. In the center of each planet is a rocky core. The core is probably as big as Earth—but is still only a small part of each planet.

In the earliest days of the solar system, when the planets were just beginning to form, the huge swirling disk surrounding the Sun varied greatly in temperature. It was hot near the Sun but very cold out where the giant planets would eventually form. This chilly part of the disk, like the hotter inner part, was made mostly of hydrogen and helium gas. But it also contained small bits of ice—ice that would have evaporated had it been nearer the Sun. The bits of ice collided and joined with bits of rock and grew to form icy planetesimals, which themselves collided and formed the beginnings of the giant planets. The growth of these planets accelerated when a wind of particles from the early Sun blew gas from the inner part of the solar system outward. As that gas reached the colder outer disk, some of it condensed into ice. Jupiter and Saturn quickly

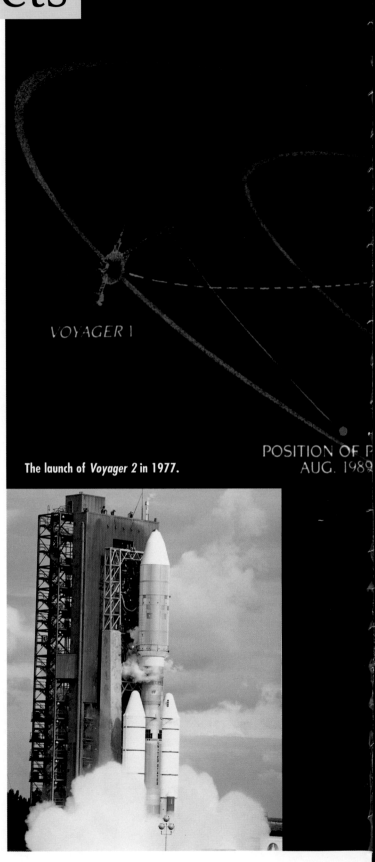

VOYAGER 1

POSITION OF P
AUG. 1989

The launch of *Voyager 2* in 1977.

In 1977, two spacecraft, *Voyager 1* and *Voyager 2,* took advantage of a rare planetary alignment — one that occurs only once every 176 years — to embark on a grand tour of the giant planets. They were able to use the gravity of one to speed them toward the next, and thereby visit all four. Both *Voyager*s flew past Jupiter and Saturn; *Voyager 2* continued on to Uranus and Neptune. By 1989, when *Voyager 2* flew past Neptune, the twin spacecraft had revolutionized our understanding of these distant worlds.

This diagram shows the orbits of Jupiter, Saturn, Uranus, and Neptune, and the paths that the two *Voyager* spacecraft followed on their grand tour of these giant planets.

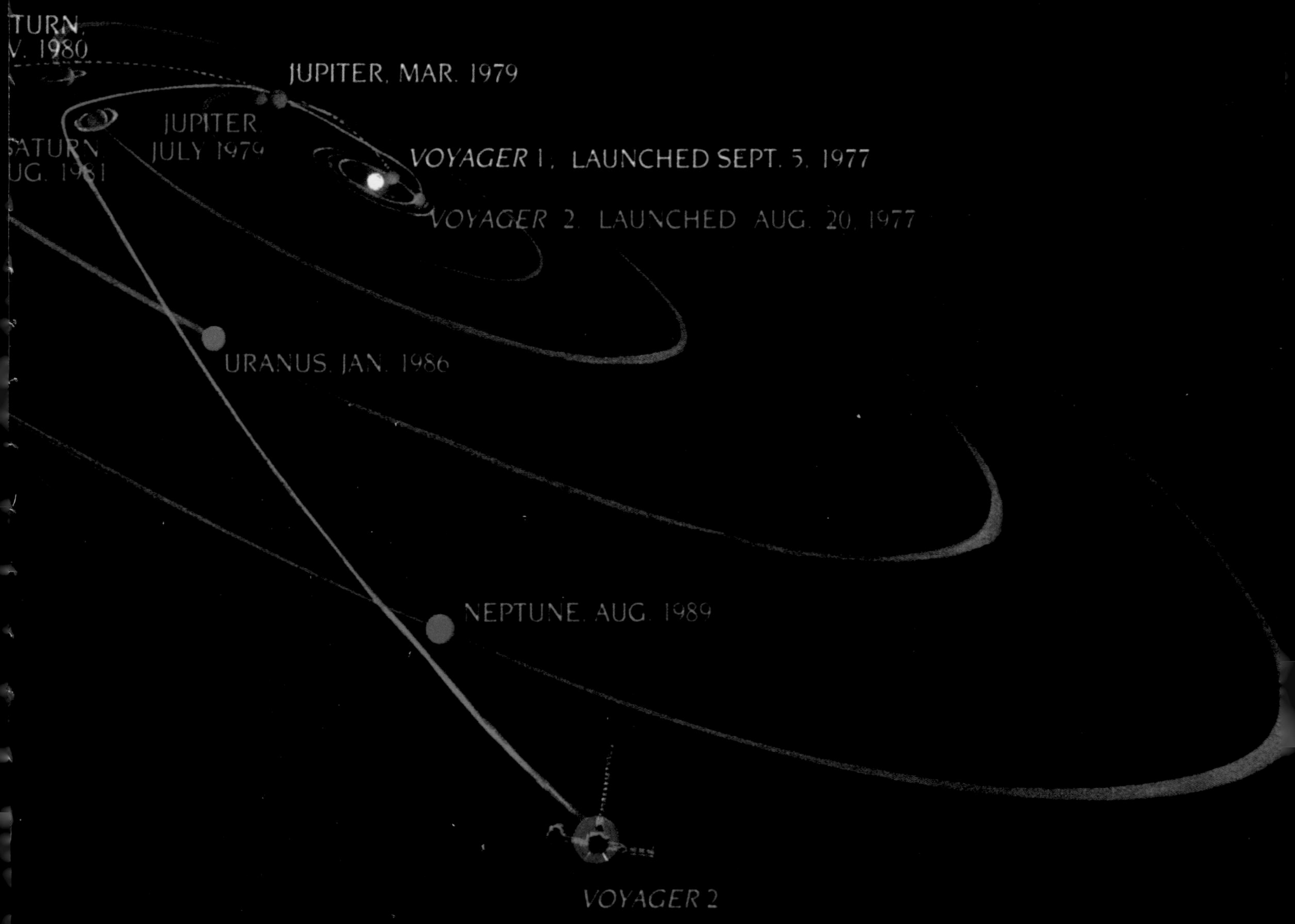

TURN.
V. 1980

JUPITER, MAR. 1979

JUPITER,
SATURN   JULY 1979
UG. 1981

VOYAGER 1, LAUNCHED SEPT. 5, 1977

VOYAGER 2, LAUNCHED AUG. 20, 1977

URANUS, JAN. 1986

NEPTUNE, AUG. 1989

VOYAGER 2

gobbled up that fresh ice and grew to twenty times the size of Earth. Their gravity was then strong enough to attract and capture the massive amounts of hydrogen and helium gas around them. They became even more enormous. Because they were able to scoop up so much of the gas in the disk, their composition became about the same as that of the disk itself. Today, Jupiter and Saturn are made mostly of hydrogen, with a significant amount of helium and only small amounts of other elements.

Uranus and Neptune were farther from the Sun and grew more slowly. By the time they became large enough for their gravity to attract the hydrogen and helium gas, most of the gas had been blown out of the solar system. These two planets became large, but not nearly as large as Jupiter and Saturn.

When the giant planets formed, they were big enough to be surrounded by disks of gas themselves. Moons formed in these disks, in much the same way that the planets had

Jupiter, Saturn, Uranus, and Neptune to scale.

formed in the disk around the Sun. These planets added other moons when their gravity captured a few planetesimals that wandered by.

Today, each of the giant planets is like a miniature solar system. Each has many moons, some very large and some very small. These moons orbit their planets much as the planets orbit the Sun.

Each of the giant planets also has a set of rings. For centuries, scientists thought that Saturn's spectacular rings were the only ones in the solar system. More recently, rings were also discovered around Jupiter, Uranus, and Neptune.

Jupiter and Saturn, the two largest giants, resemble each other in many ways. Uranus and Neptune are smaller, but still immense compared to Earth or Venus. These four huge planets differ greatly from the terrestrial worlds—and some of the moons that orbit them are among the most fascinating places in the solar system.

Jupiter

DISTANCE FROM SUN	484 million miles
ORBITAL PERIOD	11.9 Earth years
ROTATION PERIOD	9.8 hours
DIAMETER	88,846 miles (11.2 x Earth's)
MASS	318 times Earth's
TEMPERATURE (cloud tops)	-170 °F
MOONS	60 known

Pioneer 10 and *Pioneer 11* gave us our first fleeting glimpses of Jupiter in 1973 and 1974. Five years later, *Voyager 1* and *Voyager 2* photographed the planet in more detail and sent back the first closeups of its many moons.

The pictures revealed a world of bright colors and complex patterns. Jupiter's turbulent atmosphere is streaked with yellow, orange, red, and white bands of clouds and churns with violent storms. The photographs of its moons were even more stunning: instead of dull, icy, cratered worlds, the *Voyagers* found a lava-splashed Io and an icy-smooth Europa.

In 1995, the *Galileo* spacecraft arrived at Jupiter for a much longer visit: it orbited the planet for seven years. During that time, it swooped in for detailed studies of Jupiter's moons and even dropped a small probe down into Jupiter's tumultuous atmosphere.

Jupiter is made mostly of hydrogen, with some helium and only small amounts of heavier elements. The outer part of the planet is a thick layer of gas—mostly hydrogen—that is home to towering thunderclouds, raging winds, and cyclonic storms. Deeper in, as the pressure increases, the hydrogen gas is pressed into a liquid. This odd hydrogen ocean stretches far down into the planet. Still deeper, the crushing pressure squeezes the liquid into an exotic hydrogen metal. The metallic hydrogen surrounds a rocky core about the size of the Earth.

Jupiter's upper atmosphere has several layers of clouds. The highest ones, those in the

Jupiter, *the first of the giant planets, is the largest planet in our solar system. It is more massive than all the other planets combined and absolutely dwarfs the Earth. There is no way for a spacecraft to land on Jupiter because the planet doesn't have a solid surface. Its atmosphere becomes increasingly thick until it becomes a liquid. This gargantuan world, circled by faint rings and exotic moons, is the center of its own cosmic kingdom.*

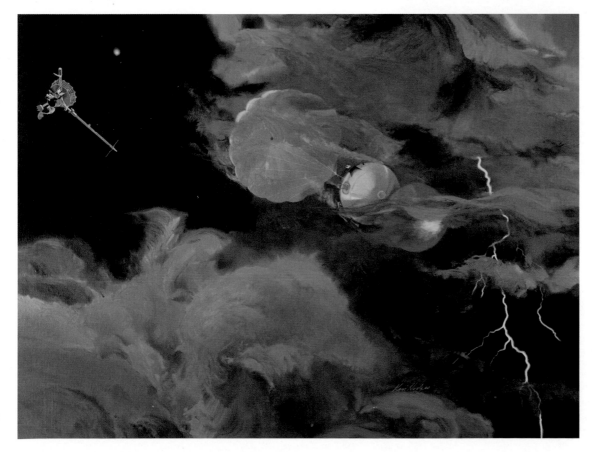

Artist's painting of the *Galileo* spacecraft and the probe that it dropped into Jupiter's atmosphere. As the probe plummeted through the clouds, it sent back data on the composition, temperature, and pressure of the atmosphere. It fell for about an hour before it was destroyed by the high pressure and extreme temperature.

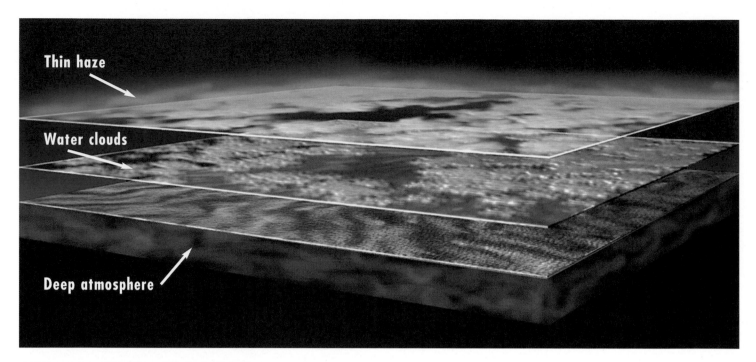

Thin haze

Water clouds

Deep atmosphere

Artist's painting of the layers of Jupiter's atmosphere.

Io, an eerie moon wracked by volcanoes and covered with lava.
(*Voyager 1*)

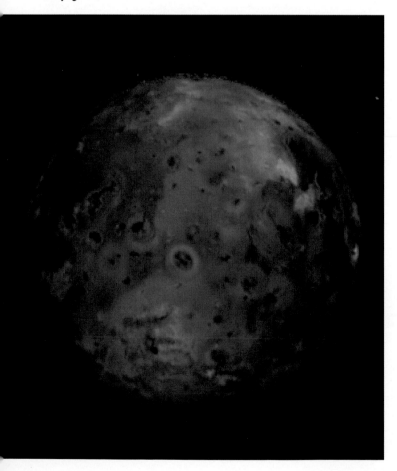

thin haze at the top, are wispy clouds of ammonia ice. A deck of water clouds lies about sixty miles below the haze. Turbulent thunderstorms build in this layer. Enormous bolts of lightning flash through the clouds, 1,000 times brighter than lightning on Earth.

Bright bands of clouds stream through the atmosphere and circle the planet. The bands are created by high-speed jet streams, strong winds blowing east to west or west to east at hundreds of miles per hour. These howling winds are powered by energy from the planet's own internal heat, not the heat from the Sun.

Jupiter's atmosphere is filled with swirling storms. Several are as big across as Earth. The most impressive is the Great Red Spot—the largest storm in the solar system. It is more than three Earths across and towers twenty miles above the clouds. It whips violently around its center, with hurricane-force winds

Jupiter's Great Red Spot. Three Earths would fit inside it. The white oval is a huge storm in Jupiter's atmosphere. (*Voyager 1*)

around its edge, and has raged in Jupiter's atmosphere for over 300 years.

Jupiter has at least thirty-nine moons that circle it the way the planets circle our Sun. They range in size from Ganymede, the largest moon in the solar system, to tiny unnamed moons less than two miles across.

Jupiter's four largest moons were discovered in 1610 by Galileo Galilei, the famous Italian scientist. When he pointed his small, handmade telescope out the window at Jupiter, he discovered four moons circling the planet. These four—Io, Europa, Ganymede, and Callisto—are sometimes known as the *Galilean moons*. The scientist's contribution to our understanding of Jupiter was honored hundreds of years later when the *Galileo* spacecraft was named after him.

Scientists expected the Galilean moons, and most other moons in the solar system, to

The handmade telescope used by Galileo in the early 1600s.

be dark, frozen, and covered with craters. They were shocked when they saw *Voyager*'s pictures of Io. There were no craters, and its surface was orange and splotchy—like a pizza hot out of the oven.

This is because Io, like all the Galilean moons, is caught in a gravitational tug of war between Jupiter and the other moons. As the moons are pushed and pulled like taffy, their insides are constantly churned and heated. Of the four, Io is the closest to Jupiter, and its insides are churned and heated the most.

Io is covered in fresh lava and wracked with volcanoes. The volcanoes throw hot gas hundreds of miles into space; so much lava flows over the moon's surface that its craters have been completely covered over. The lava bubbling out of Io is scalding—over 3,000 degrees Fahrenheit. Lava on Earth has not been that hot for at least two billion years.

A sea of molten rock seethes under the surface and feeds Io's volcanoes. One mammoth volcano, Loki, is the most energetic volcano in the solar system. Loki generates more heat than all of Earth's volcanoes combined!

Io has enormous volcanic calderas and mountains higher than any on Earth. It is covered with lava lakes and draped with

Volcanoes on Io. Right inset: a 100-mile-high plume from an erupting volcano. Left inset: the Prometheus volcano, which has been erupting almost continuously for eighteen years. The dark area is the shadow of a plume rising forty-five miles above the surface. (*Galileo*)

An active volcano on Io. The orange area on the left is flowing lava. (*Galileo*)

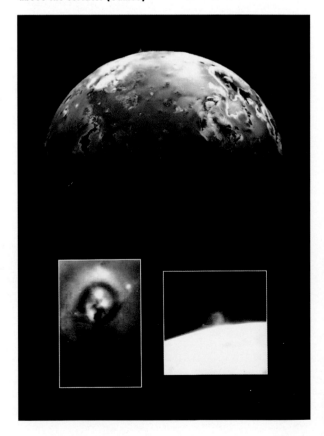

mile-high curtains of lava. It may even have a vast network of lava tubes tunneling just beneath its surface. Io is truly a bizarre world.

The next moon, Europa, is ice to Io's fire. It may be the most fascinating place in the solar system. Europa's smooth surface is a glassy layer of ice, miles thick. And, amazingly, there is a vast saltwater ocean hiding miles beneath the ice. Water—oceans of water—on a distant, icy moon of Jupiter!

On Earth, wherever there is water, there is life. Could alien microbes have evolved in the waters of Europa? All the ingredients are there. Simple organic molecules were carried to Europa long ago by the comets that pelted its surface. Hydrothermal vents, like those on Earth's seafloor, may provide an energy source and create mineral-rich environments at the bottom of its ocean.

How far have the organic chemicals in Europa's oceans evolved? Are there complex, almost-living molecules that can replicate themselves in its waters? Are there primitive living cells in its briny sea?

Scientists are planning bold missions to this intriguing moon. Eventually, a sledlike spacecraft may land on the ice, then drill miles down to get a sample of water from Europa's cold,

Europa. The bright white and bluish part of the surface is mostly water ice. The dark lines, some more than 1,800 miles long, are fractures in the ice. (*Galileo*)

A close-up of Europa's icy surface. (*Galileo*)

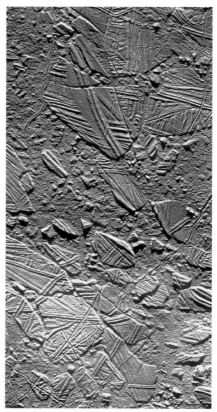

73

Artist's painting of a possible future mission to Europa. An ice-penetrating robot melts its way through the ice and releases a submersible to explore the ocean.

dark ocean. This ocean deep inside an icy moon of Jupiter is one of the very few places in our solar system that might be home to alien life.

Ganymede is the largest moon in the solar system. If it circled the Sun, not Jupiter, it would be a planet. It is bigger than Mercury and Pluto and is not much smaller than Mars.

This moon has also been warmed inside by its gravitational tug of war with Jupiter. Ganymede once had a very hot interior, and its insides are still warm enough to shape the moon. Its icy terrain is rugged and wrinkled. The frozen surface is pulled apart in places, and warmer ice occasionally rises up from below.

Ganymede, too, may have an unusual ocean beneath its surface—but one quite different from Europa's. Ganymede's salty sea begins nearly 100 miles underground and is sandwiched between two layers of ice. It is dif-

ficult to imagine sources of energy that could provide the spark for life in this dark, ice-encased ocean—but our solar system is filled with things that are difficult to imagine!

Callisto, the fourth Galilean moon, has an old, icy surface packed with thousands of craters. It looks just like scientists expected moons to look. But spacecraft measurements suggest that even this dull-looking moon may hide a salty ocean far beneath its crust.

Jupiter has at least fifty-six other moons, all much smaller than the Galilean moons. In fact, some are more like big rocks than moons! Some of them formed from material in the disk surrounding an early Jupiter; some are planetesimals that wandered too close to Jupiter and were captured by its gravity; still others are the pieces of larger moons that broke apart while circling the planet.

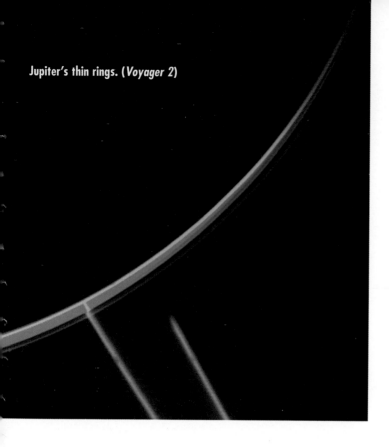
Jupiter's thin rings. (*Voyager 2*)

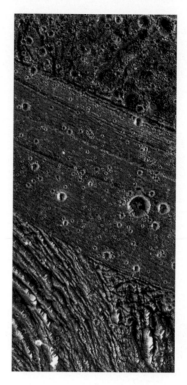
Ganymede has diverse types of terrain. The bottom section, with no craters, is the youngest. The middle section is old, with heavily cratered plains. (*Galileo*)

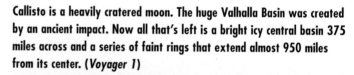
Callisto is a heavily cratered moon. The huge Valhalla Basin was created by an ancient impact. Now all that's left is a bright icy central basin 375 miles across and a series of faint rings that extend almost 950 miles from its center. (*Voyager 1*)

Several of Jupiter's small inner moons are closely related to the planet's faint rings. The rings—a faint halo ring, a slender main ring, and two very tenuous inner rings—are so thin and dark that scientists did not even know they existed until the *Voyager* spacecraft photographed them in 1979. The two inner rings appear to be made of dust particles knocked off of nearby rocky moons.

Jupiter, the massive planet with the delicate rings, is circled by some of the most interesting worlds in our solar system. When Galileo first discovered Io, Europa, Ganymede, and Callisto, he never imagined that the tiny points of light would someday be visited by a spacecraft bearing his name—or that these alien worlds would have erupting volcanoes and underground oceans that still baffle scientists today.

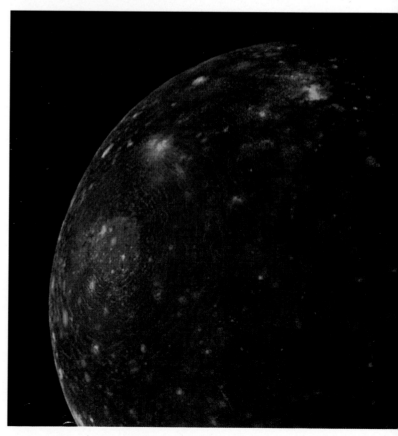

Saturn

DISTANCE FROM SUN	887 million miles
ORBITAL PERIOD	29.4 Earth years
ROTATION PERIOD	10.7 hours
DIAMETER	74,900 miles (9.5 x Earth's)
MASS	95 times Earth's
TEMPERATURE (cloud tops)	-215 °F
MOONS	31 known

Saturn was well known to even the earliest stargazers. But its true majesty wasn't revealed until the Dutch astronomer Christiaan Huygens was the first to see Saturn's rings when he peered at the planet through a small telescope in 1659. We now know that all the giant planets have rings—but none are like Saturn's.

The Sun's sixth planet is very similar to its neighbor Jupiter. It is a gigantic ball of hydrogen and helium gases surrounding a sea of liquid hydrogen and helium. The rock-and-ice core at the center of the planet is about the same size as Jupiter's (approximately the size of Earth).

Although Saturn is nearly as big across as Jupiter, it weighs only about one-third as much. The planet is very light for its size. This big ball of gas and liquid would float in an ocean of water—if you could find an ocean large enough.

From telescopes on Earth, Saturn appears to have a calm, pale yellow atmosphere. But our spacecraft showed that broad belts of yellow, brown, and orange clouds encircle the planet. The patterns are similar to those on Jupiter, but the colors are not as bright and the bands are not as sharp.

When *Voyager 1* and *Voyager 2* flew past Saturn in 1981, they sent back photographs of huge storms swirling through the planet's atmosphere. These enormous storms are not as dramatic as those on Jupiter, but they have violent winds and turbulent eddies at their edges. A roaring jet stream near Saturn's equator reaches speeds of 1,000 miles per hour.

When Saturn formed, it attracted much of the gas surrounding it. This means that it should be made of mostly hydrogen and helium, in about the same proportions as the original cloud of gas—and the Sun. But astronomers studying Saturn's atmosphere were surprised to find that it has a much lower percentage of helium than the Sun.

Scientists believe that Saturn's helium may be hidden deep inside the planet. At the temperatures and pressures in its interior, helium droplets form in the surrounding sea of liquid hydrogen. For eons, a light helium rain has been falling steadily toward the center of the planet.

Saturn *is the most majestic of our planets. This giant is second only to Jupiter in size and, like Jupiter, is made mostly of hydrogen and helium. Saturn is nearly twice as far from the Sun as Jupiter. Its long, slow journey around the Sun takes over twenty-nine years. This magical world is circled by at least thirty moons of all sizes, and its breathtaking rings have dazzled astronomers for centuries.*

A false-color image showing the bands and disturbances in Saturn's atmosphere. (Voyager 2)

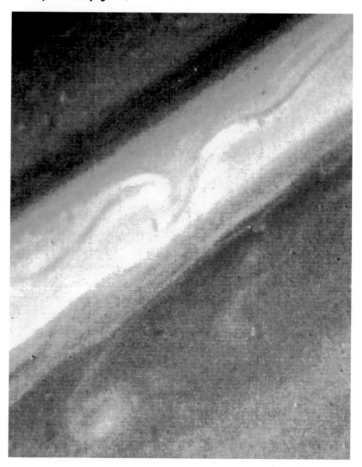

A computer-enhanced image of Saturn's magnificent rings. (*Voyager 2*)

Saturn is surrounded by a magnificent sheet of rings. The rings are made up of billions of small particles, each like a miniature moon in its own orbit around the planet. If you could scoop up all the particles that form the rings, you would have enough material to make a small moon.

For a long time scientists suspected that Saturn's rings were made of ice because they reflect most of the sunlight that strikes them. This was confirmed by telescope observations in the 1970s.

But the size of the ice particles remained unknown. To find out how big they are, scientists designed an experiment: they had the *Voyager* spacecraft transmit radio signals through the rings back to Earth. Those signals were changed as they passed through the rings. By studying the changes, scientists learned that some of the particles are as small as crystals and some are as big as a house.

It is still a mystery how rings actually form. Saturn's rings may be pieces of comets that strayed too close to the planet and were torn apart by its gravity. Or they may be all that is left of a moon shattered by a collision long ago. In either case, the fragments would have gone into orbit around Saturn and eventually settled into rings around its equator.

Saturn's rings are exquisitely thin — the distance from the top to the bottom is less than 100 feet. Titan, Saturn's largest moon, casts a shadow on the planet. (*Hubble Space Telescope*)

Some of Saturn's ring particles are affected by the gravitational forces of small moons. The painting shows two small shepherd moons keeping the particles in a slender ring.

There is one narrow ring beyond the outer edge of the main sheet of rings. The *Voyager* spacecraft discovered two tiny moons on either side of this ring that work together to keep the ring so slender. Each moon's gravity pulls the particles in opposite directions, keeping them trapped between the moons. These moons are called "shepherd moons" because they herd the ring and keep it confined. There may be more small moons that shape Saturn's other rings and sweep their edges clean.

Saturn has at least thirty moons. Some are small, oddly shaped chunks of ice. Some are medium-sized, frozen balls. And one is a large, hazy world with an atmosphere more like Earth's than any other.

Most of Saturn's moons are icy balls that formed in the disk surrounding the early planet. But some were captured by the planet

Saturn and two of its moons, Tethys and Dione. The rings cast a shadow on the planet. (*Voyager 1*)

after it formed. Phoebe is one of those. It was probably an asteroid that came too close to Saturn and was captured by the pull of the planet's gravity.

Mimas is a survivor. This small moon was once nearly shattered by a jolting collision. The impact left a crater eighty miles wide, with a mountain at its center higher than Mount Everest. If the collision had been much harder, Mimas would have split apart. A smaller

moon, Hyperion, is probably a piece of a once larger moon that wasn't so lucky.

Titan, Saturn's largest moon, is a remarkable world. Spacecraft found it hidden beneath a blanket of orange haze, a kind of smog that forms when sunlight strikes molecules high in its atmosphere. Titan is the only moon in the solar system with a substantial atmosphere. In fact, its air is thicker than our air on Earth.

The air we breathe is mostly nitrogen, with

Mimas. (*Voyager 1*)

Hyperion. (*Voyager 2*)

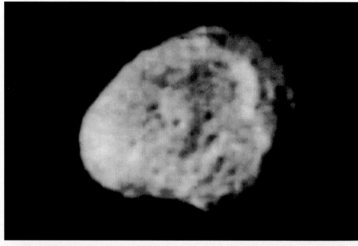

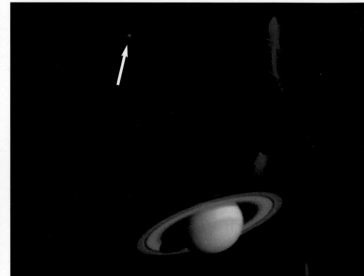

Artist's painting of a collision that breaks a moon apart and starts the formation of a ring system.

Saturn and its moon Titan. (*Cassini*)

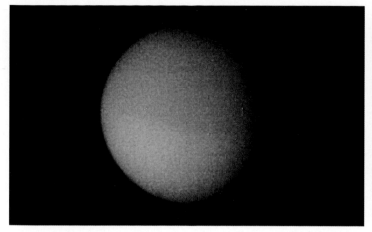

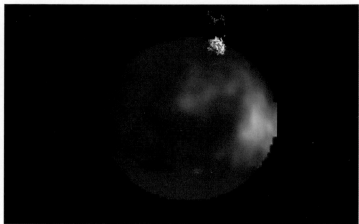

a significant amount of oxygen mixed in; Titan's air is also mostly nitrogen, but with a significant amount of methane instead. The presence of methane, and a slew of other organic molecules, makes Titan a very interesting world.

Below the orange haze, telescopes have shown bright patches that might be icy continents and dark patches that might be oceans of oily hydrocarbons—pitch-black seas of the chemicals ethane and methane. Ethane may be as common on Titan as water is on Earth. On a stormy day, dark methane clouds might produce a gentle drizzle of ethane rain. Occasional downpours might fill winding ethane rivers that feed into chilly ethane lakes.

This odd rain may create wet environments strangely similar to those on early Earth. There are literally oceans of organic molecules on Titan. What complex chemicals might exist there? Do almost-living molecules wash onto Titan's oily shores? One day, Saturn's large moon may help us to understand how complex molecules evolve into what we call life.

Top left: Saturn's largest moon, Titan, has a hazy orange atmosphere. (*Voyager 1*)

Top right: Infrared photograph of Titan. The light and dark areas may be icy continents and oceans of hydrocarbons. (*Hubble Space Telescope*)

Artist's painting shows the *Huygens* probe descending through Titan's hazy atmosphere to its icy surface. Saturn and the *Cassini* spacecraft are in the background.

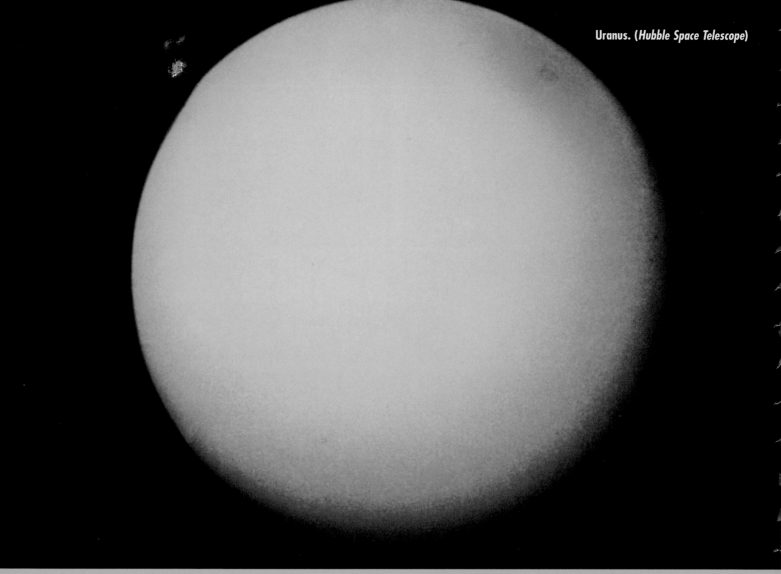

Uranus

DISTANCE FROM SUN	1.8 billion miles
ORBITAL PERIOD	83.8 Earth years
ROTATION PERIOD	17.2 hours
DIAMETER	31,763 miles (4 x Earth's)
MASS	14.5 times Earth's
TEMPERATURE (cloud tops)	-280 °F
MOONS	21 known

Two thousand years ago, children could gaze up into the night sky and chart the paths of Venus, Mars, Jupiter, and Saturn. These eager sky-watchers had no way of knowing about Uranus. It is too faint to be seen with the naked eye. In 1781, British astronomer William Herschel discovered Uranus—the first planet ever found with a telescope.

Though Uranus is a giant planet, it is not as giant as Jupiter and Saturn. Like those two planets, Uranus grew from rocky and icy planetesimals. But it didn't grow quickly enough to attract the huge amounts of hydrogen and helium that made Jupiter and Saturn so big.

Today, most of Uranus is a mixture of rock and ice. It probably has an Earth-sized rocky core surrounded by a large mantle of hot, slushy ices. Only the outer quarter of the planet is made of gas.

The atmosphere of Uranus is mostly hydrogen and helium gas, like the atmospheres of Jupiter and Saturn. It also has a small amount of methane. The methane gives Uranus its pale blue-green color. When sunlight strikes the planet's atmosphere, the methane absorbs the red and yellow light. The light we see—the light reflected from the atmosphere—looks blue-green because it is missing the yellow and red.

Uranus's atmosphere is nearly featureless. It does not have the streaming bands of color or swirling storms seen on Jupiter and Saturn. When the *Voyager 2* spacecraft flew past the planet in 1986, it measured strong winds, but not as strong as the winds on the other giants.

One of the most unusual things about Uranus is its orientation: it orbits the Sun on

Uranus, the Sun's seventh planet, lies far beyond Saturn. Only one spacecraft, Voyager 2, has ever visited this cold, distant world. Uranus is the third of the giant planets and home to eleven rings and at least twenty-one small- to medium-sized moons. The Sun, nearly two billion miles away, looks small in its sky. When Voyager sailed toward the planet, its cameras had to be adjusted to take pictures in the dim sunlight—it was like taking pictures by moonlight on Earth.

Uranus orbits the Sun on its side. First its south pole, then its north pole, is in sunlight — for forty-two years.

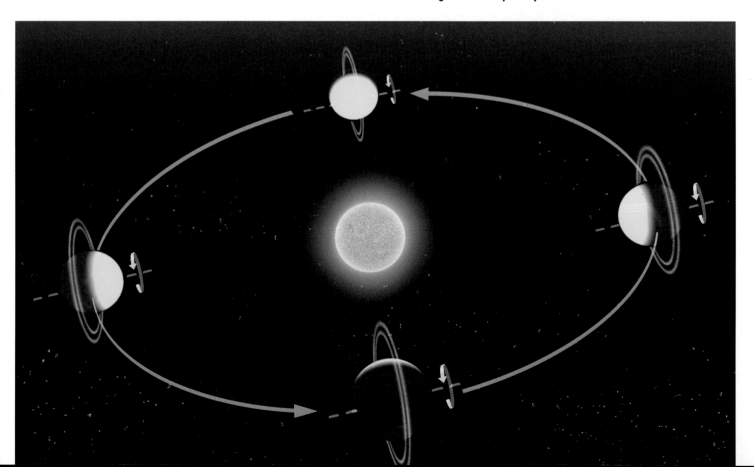

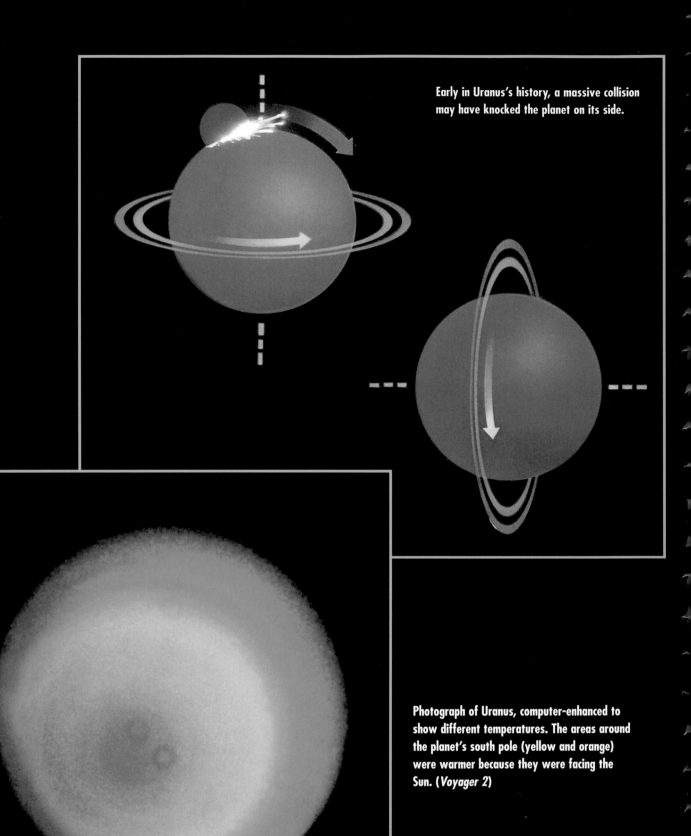

Early in Uranus's history, a massive collision may have knocked the planet on its side.

Photograph of Uranus, computer-enhanced to show different temperatures. The areas around the planet's south pole (yellow and orange) were warmer because they were facing the Sun. (*Voyager 2*)

its side. In the chaotic early days of the solar system, a huge planetesimal—as large as Earth—crashed into the planet and knocked it over. During Uranus's long eighty-four-year trip around the Sun, first its south pole, then its north pole, is in dim but constant sunlight—each pole for nearly forty-two years!

Uranus has a set of delicate rings and a collection of small- and medium-sized moons that almost certainly formed after the planet was slammed onto its side. The violent impact would have disrupted anything that was in orbit at the time of the collision.

Eleven narrow rings circle this pale blue world. They are very different from the faint rings around Jupiter and from the sparkling rings around Saturn. Uranus's rings are narrow, separated by wide gaps, and made mostly of boulder-sized chunks of dark rock and ice. They are probably shaped by shepherd moons, but so far the only shepherds that have been found are the two herding its most distant ring.

Uranus has at least twenty-one moons. All are made of ice and rock. Even the biggest, Titania, is only half the size of Earth's Moon. Five of the planet's moons were discovered

A close-up of the rings of Uranus. (Voyager 2)

through telescopes long ago. Titania and Oberon were discovered in 1789, just a few years after Uranus itself. Ariel and Umbriel were first seen in 1851, and Miranda (which is less than half the size of these others) was found nearly 100 years later. When *Voyager 2* passed by Uranus, it discovered ten small moons orbiting close to the planet. At least six more tiny moons have been detected since—some by scientists sifting through the old *Voyager* data and some by astronomers using sophisticated telescopes. There could easily be other miniature moons that we simply haven't found yet orbiting this distant planet.

Miranda is by far the oddest moon circling Uranus. It looks like a jigsaw puzzle whose pieces have been scrambled. Part of its surface looks old and cratered; part of it looks young and jagged. There are ice cliffs climbing ten miles high and canyons dropping ten miles deep. Miranda looks as though it was once torn apart by a collision, then slowly reassembled from the orbiting pieces to form the moon we see today.

Uranus and its five largest moons.

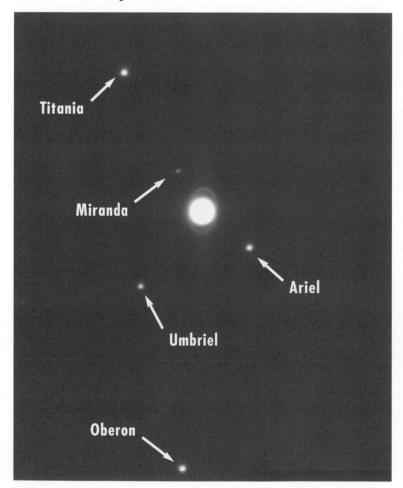

A false-color image of Uranus, showing its rings and eight of its moons. (*Hubble Space Telescope*)

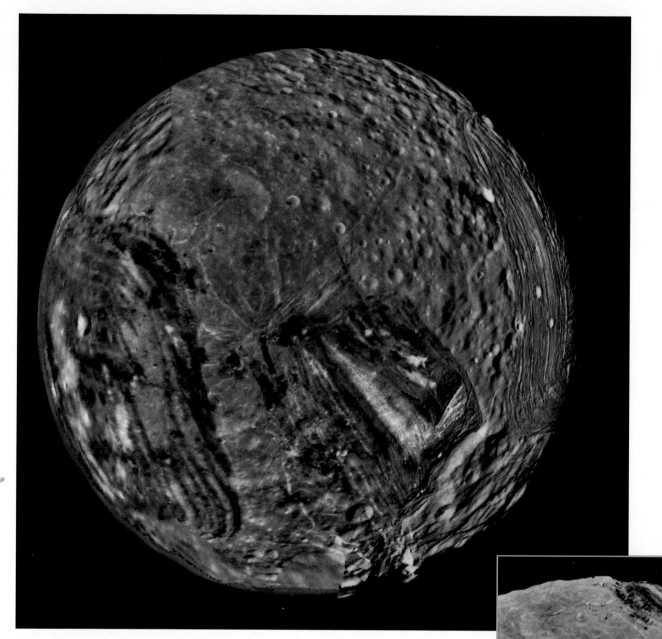

Miranda with its jumbled terrain. (*Voyager 2*)

Voyager 2, the only spacecraft to ever visit Uranus, flew past the planet in 1986. There are no spacecraft headed there now, and none are planned for at least another decade. Scientists are still analyzing the data sent back by *Voyager 2* and are studying the planet through telescopes. But it will be a long time before they get another closeup view of this distant world.

A close-up of Miranda's cliffs and canyons. (*Voyager 2*)

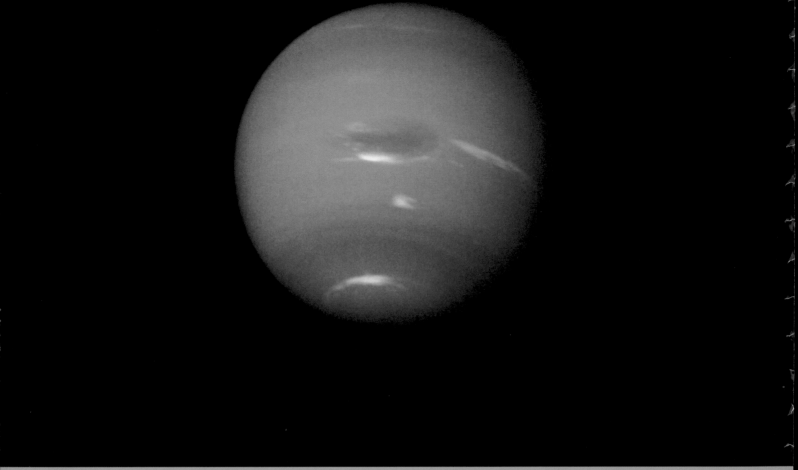

Neptune

DISTANCE FROM SUN	2.8 billion miles
ORBITAL PERIOD	164 Earth years
ROTATION PERIOD	16.1 hours
DIAMETER	30,775 miles (3.9 x Earth's)
MASS	17 times Earth's
TEMPERATURE (cloud tops)	-235 °F
MOONS	11 known

Neptune was discovered not with a telescope but with pencil and paper. In the early 1800s, astronomers carefully charted the path of Uranus as it slowly made its way around the Sun. They found that its orbit was not precisely what they predicted it to be. The difference could be explained if Uranus was being tugged by the gravity of some unknown planet even farther from the Sun.

More than sixty years after the discovery of Uranus, mathematicians calculated where this new planet should be. When astronomers turned their telescopes to that part of the sky in 1846, there was Neptune.

Voyager 2 is the only spacecraft that has ever visited Neptune. This remote world was the last stop on its grand tour of the giant planets. *Voyager's* 1989 encounter with Neptune was brief, but scientists learned more about the planet from the transmitted photographs and data than they had from all the telescope observations of the previous 100 years.

Neptune is very much like Uranus. It is only slightly smaller than its sister planet, and it has a similar composition. Neptune's thick atmosphere is made mostly of hydrogen, helium, and a little methane. Below its clouds lies a slushy layer of hot ices. Deep inside, the temperature and pressure are high enough to break methane apart into carbon and hydrogen, then to squeeze the carbon into diamond. Tiny bits of diamond may rain toward the center of Neptune just as helium droplets do on Saturn. At the very center of the planet there may be a rocky core, about the size of Earth.

This deep-blue world has violent weather. Wild storms, like those on Jupiter and Saturn,

Neptune, *the eighth planet from the Sun, is the most distant planet ever explored by spacecraft. Voyager 2 traveled twelve years to reach it. This deep-blue world is a near twin of Uranus. The two planets are about the same size, and their composition is very similar. Like all the other giant planets, Neptune is circled by a set of faint rings and a family of moons. Triton, its most famous moon, is probably a refugee from the Kuiper Belt.*

Neptune (right) is slightly smaller than Uranus (left). Its atmosphere contains a bit more methane than Uranus's does. This gives Neptune a deeper blue color.

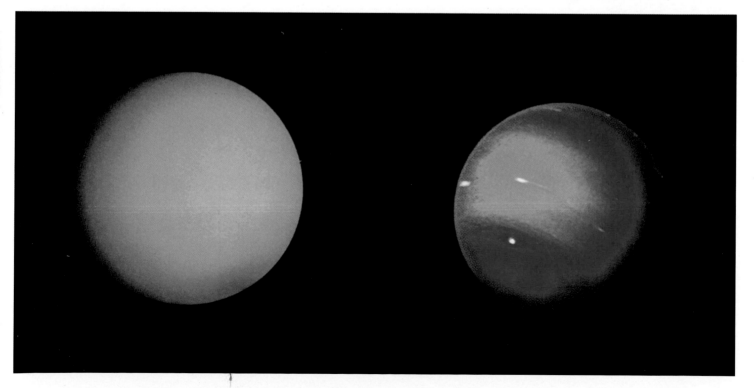

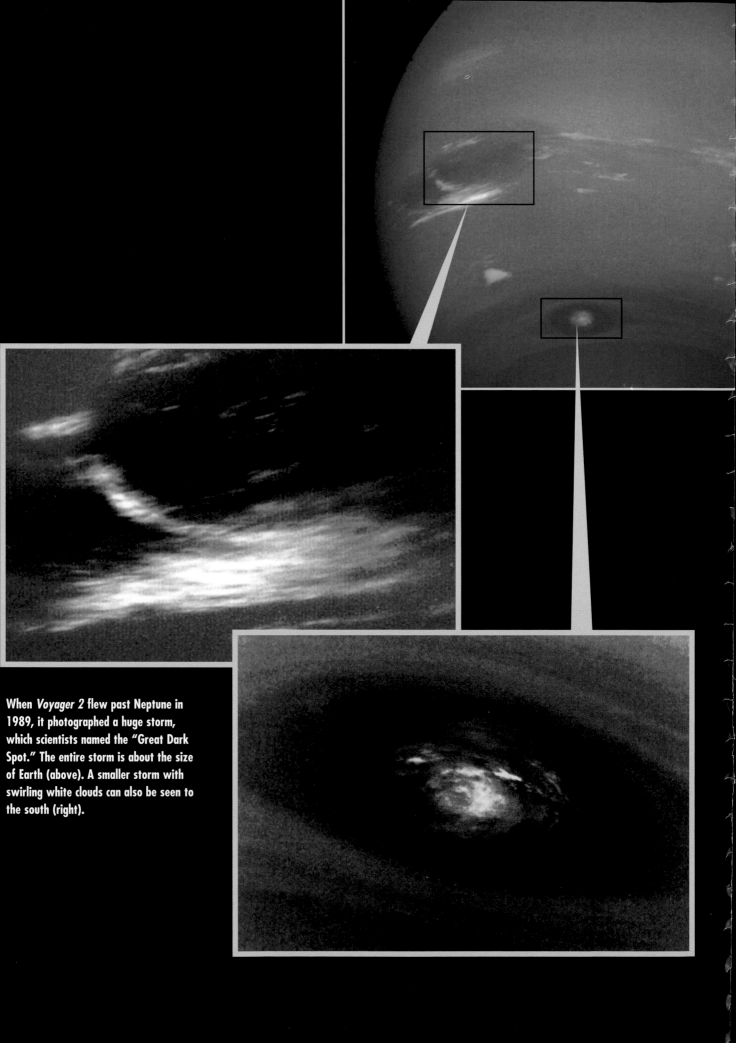

When *Voyager 2* flew past Neptune in 1989, it photographed a huge storm, which scientists named the "Great Dark Spot." The entire storm is about the size of Earth (above). A smaller storm with swirling white clouds can also be seen to the south (right).

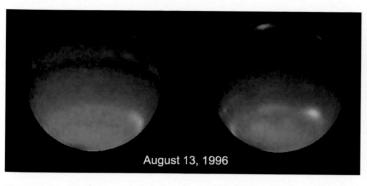
August 13, 1996

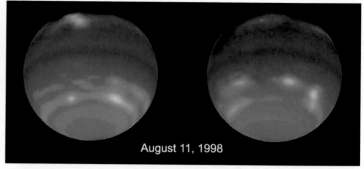
August 11, 1998

Neptune's atmosphere is always changing. A photograph taken in 1996 shows relatively calm weather. In contrast, a photograph taken in 1998 shows many storms. (*Hubble Space Telescope*)

rage in its atmosphere. *Voyager 2* photographed one huge storm about the size of Earth, with winds over 1,400 miles per hour. The storm was called the "Great Dark Spot" because it resembled Jupiter's Great Red Spot. The Great Red Spot has lasted for centuries. No one knows how long Neptune's storm lasted—but when the *Hubble Space Telescope* photographed the planet five years after *Voyager*'s visit, the storm was gone.

Five dark rings circle Neptune. The rings are very faint and can be seen from Earth only with the most powerful telescopes. Three of them are narrow, like the rings of Uranus; the other two are wider and more spread out. Neptune's outermost ring looks like it's broken in pieces—in some places it even seems to vanish. Apparently, the particles are not spread out evenly, so that some parts of the ring are thicker than others. The thicker parts can be seen through a telescope, but the thin parts cannot.

We know of eleven moons around Neptune. The largest, Triton, was discovered shortly after Neptune in 1846. One hundred

Neptune's faint rings. (*Voyager 2*)

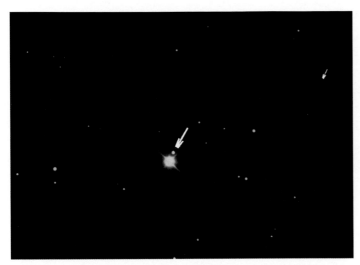

Neptune and two of its moons photographed from a large Earth-based telescope. Triton appears near the planet (large arrow), and Nereid farther away (small arrow).

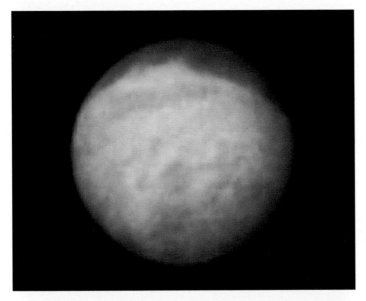

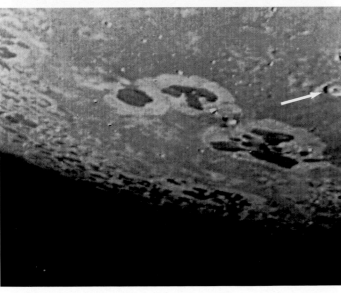

years passed before the next largest, Nereid, was seen through a telescope. Neptune's other moons are smaller and even more difficult to detect. Fifty years after astronomers found Nereid, *Voyager 2* zipped by the planet and discovered six more moons. As recently as 2003, scientists using sophisticated Earth-based telescopes detected three more.

Neptune appears to have far fewer moons than the other giant planets. But it is likely that Neptune has moons that we simply haven't discovered yet. This planet is so far away that if it has very tiny moons, like the other giant planets, they would be very difficult to detect from Earth.

The large moon Triton seems to be a misfit. Most moons form in a disk of gas that swirls around their planet shortly after the planet forms. They travel in nearly circular paths around the equator of the planet, and they orbit in the same direction as the planet spins. Triton orbits at a sharp angle to Neptune's equator, and it orbits in the wrong direction. Scientists have concluded that this moon was not formed at Neptune—it came from somewhere else.

Triton is similar to the thousands of small icy objects that orbit the Sun beyond Neptune. It probably formed in the Kuiper Belt with its cousins, the Kuiper Belt Objects. Eventually, its

Middle left: Triton, from 3.3 million miles away. (*Voyager 2*)

Bottom left: A close-up of Triton's interesting surface, showing distinct light and dark areas. A fresh crater is visible on the far right of the image. (*Voyager 2*)

orbit around the Sun brought it thundering toward Neptune. Although it missed the planet, it probably collided with one of Neptune's moons. The collision slowed Triton enough that it was captured by Neptune's gravity. It became Neptune's newest moon.

After Triton was captured, it slowly settled into its tilted, backward orbit. Neptune's gravity pulled on the moon, churning its interior and heating Triton through and through. Triton may have been a molten moon for nearly a billion years!

Today, this moon has an icy surface that is frozen solid, at a temperature of 390 degrees below zero Fahrenheit. Triton's south pole is covered by pink ice caps, and its terraced plains and mottled lands look like the skin of a frozen cantaloupe.

But Triton's insides are still warm enough to send slushy lava oozing up through fissures in the ice. Icy geysers shoot nitrogen gas miles into the air. They erupt when warm liquid nitrogen below the surface explodes through cracks in the ice—the way a warm soft drink does when you pop open the can.

Triton is one of the few moons in the solar system with an atmosphere. The air is very thin: it is made of nitrogen and methane gases, much like a thinner version of the air on Saturn's large moon, Titan. Light winds in Triton's atmosphere blow patchy clouds and wispy streamers across its cold, dark sky.

It will be years and years before another spacecraft sails all the way to Neptune. As *Voyager 2* passed the planet, it turned and snapped a parting photograph of Neptune and Triton. There won't be another picture like this taken for a very long time.

Neptune and Triton. (*Voyager 2*)

The Kuiper Belt

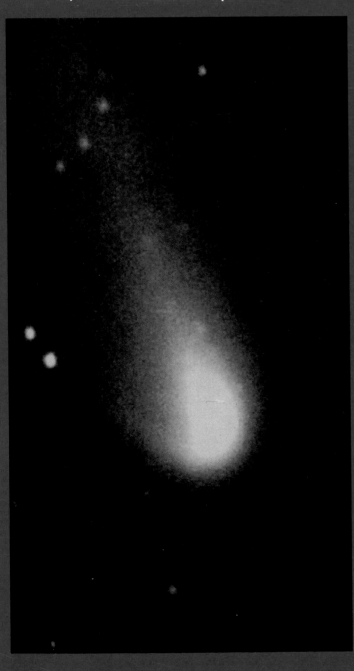

Comet Wild 2, a comet that came from the Kuiper Belt.

The Kuiper Belt is a collection of small, icy objects orbiting the Sun beyond Neptune. It was just a theory until 1992, when, after years of searching, astronomers Jane Luu and David Jewitt discovered the first Kuiper Belt Object—a tiny body, only 150 miles across, billions of miles from the Sun.

Decades earlier, Gerard Kuiper and Kenneth Edgeworth separately proposed the existence of these distant objects. It seemed unlikely to them that planetesimals would form out as far as Neptune but no farther. Each predicted that there were many, many icy planetesimals farther out in the solar system. They were right. Several hundred KBOs have been discovered since 1992, and astronomers now believe that there are many hundreds of thousands more out there.

All of the Kuiper Belt Objects are very faint—more than 100 times fainter than Pluto—which explains why it took so long to find the first one. Even the biggest are only a few hundred miles across. They are part ice, part rock, and very cold—more than 350 degrees below zero Fahrenheit.

The Kuiper Belt Objects are similar to the icy planetesimals that combined to form the cores of the giant planets. And since these

Artist's painting of several icy Kuiper Belt Objects, bodies that orbit the Sun beyond the orbit of Neptune.

frigid pieces of the ancient past haven't changed much in 4.5 billion years, they could teach us about the formation of planetesimals and about the deep interiors of the giant planets.

Pluto

DISTANCE FROM SUN	3.7 billion miles (average)
ORBITAL PERIOD	248 Earth years
ROTATION PERIOD	6.4 Earth days
DIAMETER	1,450 miles (18% of Earth's)
MASS	.2% of Earth's
TEMPERATURE (surface)	-385 °F
MOONS	1 known

For nearly a century after the discovery of Neptune, students were taught that there were eight planets in our solar system. But observations of the orbits of Uranus and Neptune led some astronomers to suspect that there might be yet one more, even farther from the Sun.

Year after year, astronomers searched the sky for "Planet X." Finally in 1930, Clyde Tombaugh, a young astronomer working at the Lowell Observatory in Arizona, found Pluto. Years later, that discovery of our ninth planet proved to be pure luck. Modern instruments don't show any of the wobbles in the orbits of Uranus and Neptune that were suggested by early observations.

Pluto's long journey around the Sun takes 248 years. Its path is different from the paths of the other planets. While their orbits are nearly circular, Pluto's is elongated. Its distance from the Sun changes slowly but dramatically. In fact, Pluto is not always our most distant planet.

When Pluto is closest to the Sun, it actually crosses inside Neptune's path. For 20 of the 248 years of its orbit Pluto is closer to the Sun than Neptune is. Though the orbits of Pluto and Neptune cross, there is no danger the two planets will ever collide. When Pluto crosses Neptune's path, Neptune is billions of miles away.

Not much is known about this mysterious planet. It is so small that even through a powerful telescope it is just a blurry little ball of light. For almost fifty years scientists did not know its size very accurately and did not realize that it had a moon.

Pluto was long considered a lonely outpost on the edge of the solar system — an odd little planet different from all others. Now we know that Pluto is a relative of the family of Kuiper Belt Objects that formed in the cold outer reaches of the solar system. This tiny planet is smaller than seven moons, including our own. It is so far from the Sun that there is almost no difference between night and day. No spacecraft has ever visited this dark, icy world, and we know very little about it.

Pluto's unusual orbit is more elongated than those of the other planets (left) and is tilted about 17 degrees out of the plane of the solar system (right). During part of its orbit, Pluto is actually closer to the Sun than Neptune (that won't happen again until the year 2227).

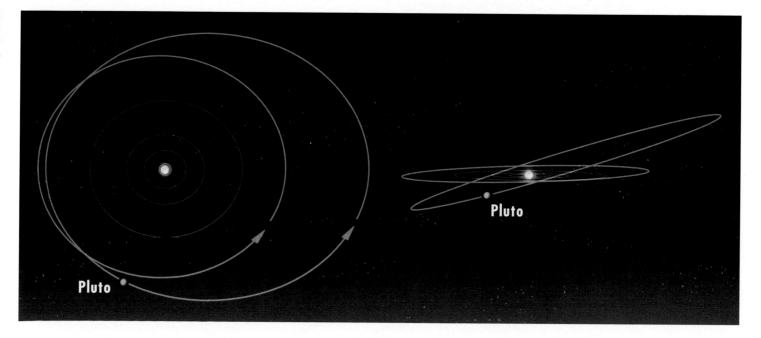

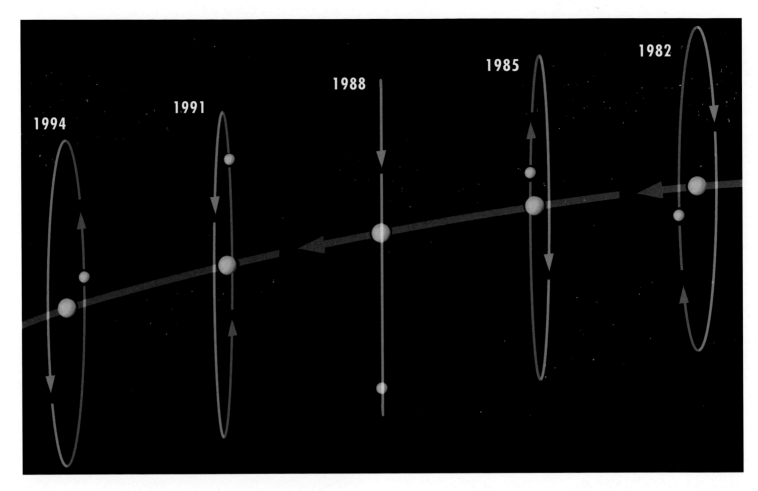

Shortly after Charon was discovered, Pluto and Charon were oriented in just the right way for astronomers to observe a series of eclipses. The sketch at the far right shows how they appeared from Earth in 1982. Charon orbits Pluto once every 6.4 days. As Pluto travels in its orbit, the geometry as seen from Earth changes. Beginning in 1985, Charon appeared to pass in front of (and then behind) a small part of Pluto. In 1988, Charon passed directly in front of, then directly behind the planet. As Charon eclipsed Pluto and then was eclipsed by it, astronomers could measure their orbits, diameters, and masses. The eclipses occurred from 1985 to 1991, and enabled scientists to learn a lot about both worlds.

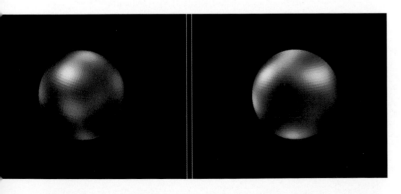

Our best views of Pluto's surface. The blurry images show ice caps at the southern and northern poles and extensive dark regions near the equator. (*Hubble Space Telescope*)

In 1978, astronomers discovered Pluto's moon, Charon. By a fortunate circumstance, this helped them learn more about Pluto itself. A few years later, Pluto and Charon were oriented in just the right way that they eclipsed each other when viewed from Earth. The eclipses allowed astronomers to accurately measure the orbit, size, and mass of both Pluto and its moon.

Pluto is only about 1,400 miles across, one-fifth the size of Earth and smaller than our Moon. This cold ball of rock and ice is covered with an exotic frost of nitrogen, methane, and carbon monoxide. The frost gives the planet a reddish tint.

For decades Pluto was thought to be an

unusual loner, orbiting by itself beyond the giant planets. Recently, scientists discovered that Pluto is not unusual and it is not alone. There are thousands and thousands of small, icy Kuiper Belt Objects orbiting the Sun in this distant part of the solar system. Pluto was born among the icy planetesimals of the Kuiper Belt and is a large relative of the smaller Kuiper Belt Objects.

Had astronomers known about the thousands of Kuiper Belt Objects when Pluto was discovered, they might have classified Pluto as one of them. But in 1930, because nobody knew about the Kuiper Belt Objects, Pluto was called a planet. By the time the Kuiper Belt Objects were discovered six decades later, the world was so used to thinking of Pluto as a planet that scientists decided not to change its status.

Pluto's closest relative in the solar system may be Neptune's moon Triton. It is likely that both originated in the Kuiper Belt. They are about the same size (Triton is slightly larger) and are both made of approximately two-thirds rock and one-third ice: the composition scientists expect for objects that formed beyond Neptune.

Like Triton, Pluto has a thin atmosphere made mostly of nitrogen gas. Evidence of its atmosphere was found in 1988, when Pluto passed directly in front of a bright star. As Pluto moved slowly in front of the star, the light from the star gradually dimmed. The light dimmed because it was passing through

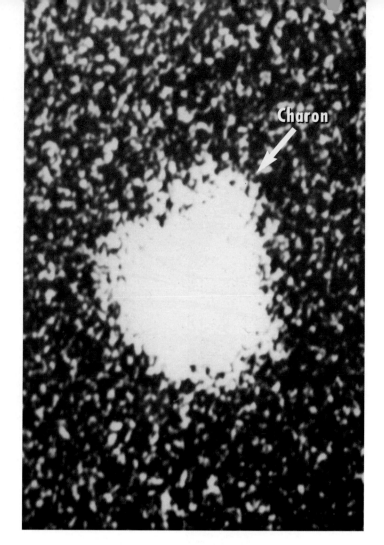

Pluto's moon, Charon, was discovered in this image. It looks like a small bump on Pluto.

Pluto's atmosphere on its way to our telescopes. When the edge of the planet's surface moved in front of the star, the light was blocked completely. The gradual dimming at the beginning of the eclipse was proof that Pluto has an atmosphere.

Pluto's orbit is now taking it farther from the Sun. It is possible that, as its temperature drops, its atmosphere may freeze out onto its surface. Pluto may have an atmosphere only during the "warm" part of its orbit. It will be interesting to watch this world over the next

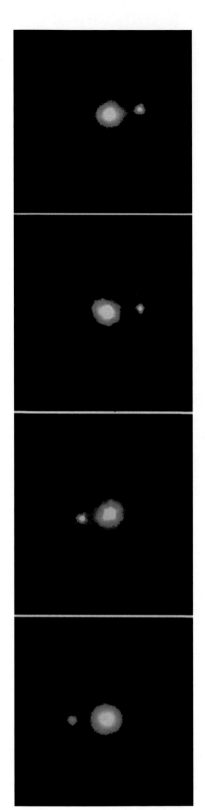

Pluto and Charon.
(Hubble Space Telescope)

Artist's painting of the frigid surface of Pluto, with Charon and the Sun visible in the sky.

few decades to see whether its atmosphere disappears.

Although Pluto is a tiny planet, it has a large moon. Most moons are much smaller than their planets, but Charon is more than half the size of Pluto.

Not only is Charon big, but it is very close to Pluto — twenty times closer than our Moon is to us. It is even closer to Pluto than most communications satellites are to Earth. The two worlds look more like a double planet than a planet and moon. If you were standing on Pluto's frosty surface, Charon would look seven times bigger than our Moon does in our sky.

As a result of the pull of gravity between Pluto and Charon, the motions of the planet

and its moon are completely synchronized. This happened over a long period of time. Charon now orbits Pluto once every 6.4 days. In exactly that same time, Pluto spins around once and Charon spins around once. They move like two people facing each other, holding hands and twirling around. The same side of Charon always faces Pluto—and the same side of Pluto always faces Charon.

Charon most likely formed in much the same way that our Moon did. Scientists believe that a large icy planetesimal, larger than Charon is today, smashed into Pluto. The collision rocked the planet and sent debris flying. Some pieces remained in orbit around Pluto and quickly coalesced to form Charon.

This same collision may have knocked Pluto over. It, like Uranus, orbits the Sun nearly on its side.

We know very little about Charon. We do know that this mysterious moon contains less rock and more ice than Pluto and that its surface doesn't have the same reddish tinge. Unlike Pluto, Charon is covered with water ice; it has no dusting of nitrogen or methane frost, and there appear to be watery eruptions through its icy crust.

We know less about Pluto than any other planet. No spacecraft has ever visited this dark little world. None will reach it until at least 2015. Pluto and Charon will remain mysterious for years to come.

Conclusion

The Earth and its Moon. (*Galileo,* on its way to Jupiter)

Before the Space Age, people's imaginations ran wild, creating exotic visions of what our neighboring planets might look like: Venus covered with lush tropical jungles or Mars crisscrossed with water canals.

Now our spacecraft have visited every planet except Pluto. They have shown that there are no jungles on Venus and no canals on Mars. But the planets of our solar system, and their odd assortment of moons, are even more extraordinary than had been imagined.

Today, astronomers, planetary scientists, and astrobiologists sift through data, trying to answer one of the most intriguing questions of our time: Is there life anyplace besides Earth? Our planet was a perfect incubator. Life began shortly after the oceans formed. It adapted as conditions changed, and it survived. But is Earth the only place where life blossomed, or did it begin on Mars, too? What about Europa? Did primitive organisms bubble to life in its vast underground ocean? And Titan...might future spacecraft find the promise of life in the molecules on this moon of Saturn?

Our solar system is a fascinating place. Spacecraft, scientists, and astronauts will continue to explore it for decades to come. It is up to us, as the only intelligent inhabitants of our solar system, to uncover the secrets of how it began, how its worlds evolved, and how our own world came to be so special.

Artist's painting of future astronauts exploring Mars.

Glossary

asteroids: Small rocky objects that orbit the Sun. Thousands of asteroids orbit in a region called the Asteroid Belt, which lies between the orbits of Mars and Jupiter. However, some have been found in other orbits, including some that cross Earth's orbit.

Asteroid Belt: The region between the orbits of Mars and Jupiter where most asteroids are found.

astrobiologist: A scientist who studies the origin and evolution of life on Earth and the posibility of chemical evolution of primitive life elsewhere in the solar system.

astronomer: A scientist who studies celestial bodies, including planets, stars, galaxies, and other astronomical objects.

atmosphere: A layer of gas surrounding a planet or moon, held in place by the force of gravity.

bacteria (*bacterium,* singular): Microscopic organisms with a single cell and no organized cell structures.

chromosphere: The Sun's lower atmosphere, which lies just above the photosphere.

core: The central region of any planet, star, or moon.

corona: The faint upper atmosphere of the Sun, which lies just above the chromosphere.

crater: A bowl-shaped depression on the surface of a planet or moon caused by the impact of another body such as an asteroid or comet.

crust: The relatively thin, solid outer layer of a terrestrial planet or a moon.

eclipse: The phenomenon during which one celestial body passes in front of another, causing the light from the hidden body to be blocked.

electromagnetic radiation: Waves made of oscillating electric and magnetic fields that travel at the speed of light. Radio waves, infrared radiation, visible light, ultraviolet light, and X-rays are all types of electromagnetic radiation. Radio waves have the lowest energy and longest wavelengths, X-rays the highest energy and shortest wavelengths.

Fahrenheit: A temperature scale. On this scale, the freezing point of water is 32°F, the boiling point of water is 212°F, and the interval between is divided into 180 equal parts called degrees Fahrenheit.

galaxy: A large collection of stars bound together by gravity. Our Sun is one of many stars in the Milky Way galaxy.

giant planets: Jupiter, Saturn, Uranus, and Neptune. They are called the giant planets because they are so much larger than the other planets in the solar system.

gravity: The attractive force that any object with mass has on all other objects with mass. The greater the mass of the object, the stronger its gravitational pull.

greenhouse effect: The warming that occurs when certain gases (greenhouse gases) are present in a planet's atmosphere. Visible light from the Sun penetrates the atmosphere of a planet and heats the ground; the warmed ground then radiates infrared radiation back toward space. If greenhouse gases are present, they absorb some of that radiation, trapping it and making the planet warmer than it otherwise would be.

greenhouse gases: Gases such as carbon dioxide and water vapor that absorb infrared radiation. When these gases are present in a planet's atmosphere, they absorb some of the heat trying to escape the planet instead of letting it pass through the atmosphere, resulting in a greenhouse effect.

infrared radiation: A type of electromagnetic radiation with wavelengths shorter than radio waves but longer than visible light.

interstellar: The space between stars in a galaxy.

Kuiper Belt: The region beyond the orbit of Neptune where thousands of small, icy objects orbit the Sun.

Kuiper Belt Objects: The small, icy objects that orbit the Sun in the Kuiper Belt.

lava: Molten rock that has risen through a planet's crust and spilled onto the surface.

magma: Molten rock beneath a planet's crust.

mantle: The layer of molten rock surrounding a terrestrial planet's core.

mass extinction: The disappearance of many species of living things at the same time due to a global catastrophe.

microscopic organism (also known as *microbe*): A form of life, usually single-celled, that is too small to be seen without a microscope.

Milky Way: Our own galaxy. It has a spiral shape, and our Sun is one of its billions of stars.

moon: A small body in orbit around a planet.

nuclear fusion: The process of combining light atoms to form heavier atoms, releasing energy as a result. This requires extreme conditions, like those in the core of the Sun, where the temperature and pressure are so high that hydrogen atoms collide with enough force to form helium. The energy released powers the Sun.

Oort Cloud: A spherical collection of icy bodies that surrounds the solar system. It extends to great distances and is where most comets come from.

orbit: The path of one body around another, as a result of the force of gravity between them. Examples are a planet's path around the Sun or a moon's path around a planet.

orbital period: The amount of time it takes a body to complete one orbit around another body. Examples are the time it takes a planet to complete one orbit around the Sun or a moon to travel once around a planet.

photosphere: The Sun's visible surface layer of gas.

photosynthesis: The process by which plants use energy from sunlight to convert carbon dioxide and water into food (in the form of sugar). Oxygen is released in the process.

planet: In our solar system, one of the nine major bodies that orbit the Sun. More generally, a celestial body that orbits a star and is big enough that its gravity has pulled it into a spherical shape.

planetesimals: Objects the size of small moons that formed in the early solar system. Some combined to form the planets; others formed asteroids, comets, or Kuiper Belt Objects.

plate tectonics: The Earth's crust is broken into large sections called plates. Plate tectonics describes their constant motion relative to each other and explains the geologic activity and recycling of the crust that occurs as a result.

radar: Acronym for RAdio Detection And Ranging. A radar device bounces radio waves off a distant object, then receives and analyzes the reflected waves to determine the location and speed of the object.

radio waves: Low-energy, long-wavelength electromagnetic radiation.

rotation period: The amount of time it takes for an object to spin once on its axis.

solar flare: An explosion of particles streaming out from a region of the Sun.

solar prominence: A huge arc of glowing gas erupting from the Sun. It can hover above the photosphere for days before collapsing back to the surface.

solar wind: A stream of high-energy particles that flows outward from the Sun into the solar system.

star: A ball of hot gas held together by its gravity and generating energy through nuclear fusion in its core.

sunspot: A dark spot on the surface of the Sun. Sunspots appear dark because they are cooler than the area around them.

telescope: An instrument used to collect and focus light to produce a magnified image of a faraway object.

terrestrial planets: Mercury, Venus, Earth, and Mars. They are called the terrestrial planets because their chemical and physical properties are similar to Earth's.

topography: The position and elevation of the features of a surface, like a planet or moon.

ultraviolet light: Electromagnetic radiation with wavelengths shorter than visible light but longer than X-rays.

visible light: The small portion of the electromagnetic spectrum that our eyes can detect; electromagnetic radiation composed of all the colors of the rainbow.

X-rays: High-energy electromagnetic radiation of very short wavelengths.

Space Flights

SPACECRAFT	SOURCE	LAUNCH	TARGET	MISSION	NOTES
Luna 1	USSR	Jan. 2, 1959	Moon	flyby	Flew by Moon
Luna 3	USSR	Oct. 4, 1959	Moon	flyby	Photographed far side of Moon
OSO 1	USA	Mar. 7, 1962	Sun	orbiter	Solar observatory in Earth orbit
Mariner 2	USA	Aug. 27, 1962	Venus	flyby	Flew by Venus at 34,745-km range
Ranger 7	USA	July 28, 1964	Moon	impact	Impacted Moon—returned 4,308 photos
Mariner 4	USA	Nov. 28, 1964	Mars	flyby	Flew by Mars July 15, 1965—returned 21 photos
OSO 2	USA	Feb. 3, 1965	Sun	orbiter	Solar observatory in Earth orbit
Ranger 8	USA	Feb. 17, 1965	Moon	impact	Impacted Moon—returned 7,137 photos
Ranger 9	USA	Mar. 21, 1965	Moon	impact	Impacted Moon—returned 5,814 photos
Zond 3	USSR	June 18, 1965	Mars	test	Flew by Moon as test of Mars spacecraft
Luna 9	USSR	Jan. 31, 1966	Moon	lander	First lunar soft landing—returned photos
Luna 10	USSR	Mar. 31, 1966	Moon	orbiter	First successful lunar orbiter
Surveyor 1	USA	May 30, 1966	Moon	lander	Lunar soft landing—returned 11,150 photos
Lunar Orbiter 1	USA	Aug. 10, 1966	Moon	orbiter	Lunar photographic mapping
Pioneer 7	USA	Aug. 17, 1966	Solar wind	interplanetary	Monitored solar wind
Luna 11	USSR	Aug. 24, 1966	Moon	orbiter	Lunar-orbit science mission
Luna 12	USSR	Oct. 22, 1966	Moon	orbiter	Lunar photographic mapping
Lunar Orbiter 2	USA	Nov. 6, 1966	Moon	orbiter	Lunar photographic mapping
Luna 13	USSR	Dec. 21, 1966	Moon	lander	Soft-lander science mission
Lunar Orbiter 3	USA	Feb. 4, 1967	Moon	orbiter	Lunar photographic mapping
Surveyor 3	USA	Apr. 17, 1967	Moon	lander	Surface science mission
Lunar Orbiter 4	USA	May 4, 1967	Moon	orbiter	Photographic mapping
Venera 4	USSR	June 12, 1967	Venus	probe	Successful atmospheric probe: Oct. 18, 1967
Mariner 5	USA	June 14, 1967	Venus	flyby	Flew by Venus
Lunar Orbiter 5	USA	Aug. 1, 1967	Moon	orbiter	Photographic mapping
Surveyor 6	USA	Nov. 7, 1967	Moon	lander	Lunar-surface science mission
Pioneer 8	USA	Dec. 13, 1967	Solar wind	interplanetary	Monitored solar wind
Surveyor 7	USA	Jan. 7, 1968	Moon	lander	Lunar-surface science mission
Zond 4	USSR	Mar. 2, 1968	Moon	test	Robotic test of Soyuz lunar craft
Luna 14	USSR	Apr. 7, 1968	Moon	orbiter	Mapped lunar gravity field
Zond 5	USSR	Sept. 14, 1968	Moon	test	Circumlunar flyby—spacecraft recovered
Pioneer 9	USA	Nov. 8, 1968	Solar wind	interplanetary	Monitored solar wind
Zond 6	USSR	Nov. 10, 1968	Moon	test	Lunar flyby—precursor to human flight
Apollo 8	USA	Dec. 21, 1968	Moon	human	Human lunar orbiter and return
Venera 5	USSR	Jan. 5, 1969	Venus	probe	Atmospheric-entry probe
Venera 6	USSR	Jan. 10, 1969	Venus	probe	Atmospheric-entry probe
OSO 5	USA	Jan. 22, 1969	Sun	orbiter	Solar observatory in Earth orbit
Mariner 6	USA	Feb. 24, 1969	Mars	flyby	Flew by July 31, 1969—returned 75 photos
Mariner 7	USA	Mar. 27, 1969	Mars	flyby	Flew by Aug. 5, 1969—returned 126 photos
Apollo 10	USA	May 18, 1969	Moon	human	Human lunar orbit test—precursor to landing
Apollo 11	USA	July 16, 1969	Moon	human	First human lunar landing and return
Zond 7	USSR	Aug. 8, 1969	Moon	test	Robotic circumlunar flight and return
OSO 6	USA	Aug. 9, 1969	Sun	orbiter	Solar observatory in Earth orbit
Kosmos 300	USSR	Sept. 23, 1969	Moon	test	Possible test of Earth-orbit lunar equipment
OSO 7	USA	Sept. 29, 1971	Sun	orbiter	Solar observatory in Earth orbit
Apollo 12	USA	Nov. 14, 1969	Moon	human	Human lunar landing and return
Apollo 13	USA	Apr. 11, 1970	Moon	human	Aborted lunar landing—crew returned safely
Venera 7	USSR	Aug. 17, 1970	Venus	lander	First successful lander on Venus
Luna 16	USSR	Sept. 12, 1970	Moon	return	Lunar-surface sample return
Zond 8	USSR	Oct. 20, 1970	Moon	test	Robotic circumlunar flight and return
Luna 17	USSR	Nov. 10, 1970	Moon	rover	Robotic lunar rover: Lunokhod 1
Apollo 14	USA	Jan. 31, 1971	Moon	lander	Human lunar landing and return
Mars 2	USSR	May 19, 1971	Mars	orbiter	First Mars orbiter
Mars 3	USSR	May 28, 1971	Mars	orbiter	Orbited Mars
Mariner 9	USA	May 30, 1971	Mars	orbiter	Orbital photographic mapping
Apollo 15	USA	July 26, 1971	Moon	lander	Human lunar landing and return
Luna 19	USSR	Sept. 28, 1971	Moon	orbiter	Orbital photographic mapping
Luna 20	USSR	Feb. 14, 1972	Moon	return	Lunar-surface sample return
Pioneer 10	USA	Mar. 3, 1972	Jupiter	flyby	Flew by Jupiter
Venera 8	USSR	Mar. 27, 1972	Venus	lander	Landed on Venus

SPACECRAFT	SOURCE	LAUNCH	TARGET	MISSION	NOTES
Apollo 16	USA	Apr. 16, 1972	Moon	human	Human lunar landing and return
Apollo 17	USA	Dec. 7, 1972	Moon	human	Human lunar landing and return
Luna 21	USSR	Jan. 8, 1973	Moon	rover	Robotic lunar rover: Lunokhod 2
Pioneer 11	USA	Apr. 6, 1973	Jupiter	flyby	Flew by Jupiter
			Saturn	flyby	Flew by Saturn
Explorer 49	USA	June 10, 1973	Moon	orbiter	Solar- and galactic-radio science experiment
Mars 5	USSR	July 25, 1973	Mars	orbiter	Orbited Mars
Mariner 10	USA	Nov. 3, 1973	Venus	flyby	Flew by Venus en route to Mercury
			Mercury	flyby	Flew by Mercury three times in 1974
Luna 22	USSR	May 29, 1974	Moon	orbiter	Photographic mapping
Venera 9	USSR	June 8, 1975	Venus	lander	Landed on Venus
Venera 9 orbiter	USSR	June 8, 1975	Venus	orbiter	Orbited Venus
Venera 10	USSR	June 14, 1975	Venus	lander	Landed on Venus
Venera 10 orbiter	USSR	June 14, 1975	Venus	orbiter	Orbited Venus
OSO 8	USA	June 21, 1975	Sun	orbiter	Solar observatory in Earth orbit
Viking 1	USA	Aug. 20, 1975	Mars	orbiter	Orbited Mars
Viking 1 lander	USA	Aug. 20, 1975	Mars	lander	Landed on Mars
Viking 2	USA	Sept. 9, 1975	Mars	orbiter	Orbited Mars
Viking 2 lander	USA	Sept. 9, 1975	Mars	lander	Landed on Mars
Luna 24	USSR	Aug. 9, 1976	Moon	return	Lunar-surface sample return
Voyager 2	USA	Aug. 20, 1977	Jupiter	flyby	Flew by Jupiter
			Saturn	flyby	Flew by Saturn
			Uranus	flyby	Flew by Uranus
			Neptune	flyby	Flew by Neptune
Voyager 1	USA	Sept. 5, 1977	Jupiter	flyby	Flew by Jupiter
			Saturn	flyby	Flew by Saturn
Pioneer 12	USA	May 20, 1978	Venus	orbiter	Orbited Venus
Pioneer 13	USA	Aug. 8, 1978	Venus	probes	Four atmospheric-entry probes
Venera 11	USSR	Sept. 9, 1978	Venus	lander	Landed on Venus
Venera 12	USSR	Sept. 14, 1978	Venus	lander	Landed on Venus
Solar Max	USA	Feb. 14, 1980	Sun	orbiter	Solar observatory in Earth orbit
Venera 13	USSR	Oct. 30, 1981	Venus	lander	Landed on Venus
Venera 14	USSR	Nov. 4, 1981	Venus	lander	Landed on Venus
Venera 15	USSR	June 2, 1983	Venus	orbiter	Orbited Venus
Venera 16	USSR	June 7, 1983	Venus	orbiter	Orbited Venus
Vega 1	USSR	Dec. 15, 1984	Venus	lander	Landed on Venus
			Venus	balloon	Deployed in Venus atmosphere
			Halley	flyby	Flew by Comet Halley
Vega 2	USSR	Dec. 21, 1984	Venus	lander	Landed on Venus
			Venus	balloon	Deployed in Venus atmosphere
			Halley	flyby	Flew by Comet Halley
Sakigake	Japan	Jan. 7, 1985	Halley	flyby	Distant flyby of Comet Halley
Suisei	Japan	Aug. 18, 1985	Halley	flyby	Flew by Comet Halley
Giotto	European Space Agency (ESA)	July 2, 1985	Halley	flyby	Flew by Comet Halley
Magellan	USA	May 5, 1989	Venus	orbiter	Orbited Venus
Galileo orbiter	USA	Oct. 18, 1989	Jupiter	orbiter	Flew by Venus
					Flew by Earth
					Flew by asteroid Gaspra
					Flew by asteroid Ida
					Orbited Jupiter
Galileo probe	USA	Oct. 18, 1989	Jupiter	probe	Entered Jupiter's atmosphere
Hiten	Japan	Jan. 24, 1990	Moon	flyby	Flew by Moon
Hagoromo	Japan	Jan. 24, 1990	Moon	orbiter	Deployed into lunar orbit
Hubble Space Telescope	USA/ESA	Apr. 25, 1990	All	orbiter	2.4-meter telescope in Earth orbit
Ulysses	ESA/USA	Oct. 6, 1990	Sun	orbiter	Deployed into solar polar orbit by Jupiter flyby
Yokhoh	Japan	Aug. 30, 1991	Sun	orbiter	Solar observatory in Earth orbit
Clementine	USA	Jan. 25, 1994	Moon	orbiter	Orbited Moon
Solar and Heliospheric Observatory	ESA	Dec. 2, 1995	Sun	orbiter	Solar observatory in Earth orbit
Near Earth Asteroid Rendezvous (NEAR)	USA	Feb. 17, 1996	Eros	orbiter	Flew by asteroid Mathilde, orbited asteroid Eros for one year before landing on it
Mars Global Surveyor	USA	Nov. 7, 1996	Mars	orbiter	Orbiting Mars
Mars Pathfinder	USA	Dec. 2, 1996	Mars	lander/rover	Landed on Mars, deployed rover Sojourner
Cassini	USA	Oct. 15, 1997	Saturn	orbiter/probe	En route to Saturn
Lunar Prospector	USA	Jan. 6, 1998	Moon	orbiter	Orbited Moon
Odyssey	USA	Apr. 17, 2001	Mars	orbiter	Orbiting Mars

Planets at a Glance

PLANET	AVERAGE DISTANCE FROM SUN (AU*)	TEMPERATURE (FAHRENHEIT)	DIAMETER (MILES)	COMPOSITION	KNOWN MOONS	RINGS
Mercury	.39	(surface range) −300 to +800	3,031	Rocks, metals	0	No
Venus	.72	(surface) 850	7,520	Rocks, metals	0	No
Earth	1	(surface range) −125 to +130	7,926	Rocks, metals	1	No
Mars	1.5	(surface range) −190 to +60	4,217	Rocks, metals	2	No
Jupiter	5.2	(at cloud tops) −170	88,846	Hydrogen, helium, hydrogen compounds	60	Yes
Saturn	9.5	(at cloud tops) −215	74,900	Hydrogen, helium, hydrogen compounds	31	Yes
Uranus	19.2	(at cloud tops) −280	31,763	Hydrogen, helium, hydrogen compounds	21	Yes
Neptune	30.1	(at cloud tops) −235	30,775	Hydrogen, helium, hydrogen compounds	11	Yes
Pluto	39.5	(surface) −385	1,450	Ices, rocks	1	No

*AU = astronomical unit. (The distance between the Earth and the Sun.)

J. Kelly Beatty/Sky Pub: p. 29 bottom

Bettmann/CORBIS: p. 71 bottom

Tom Brock: p. 57 top

Don Dixon: p. 70 top

Elizabeth Frenchman: pp. 62–63 center

John Harmon/NAIC: p. 24 bottom

John Hartmann: pp. 100–101

W. Hartmann: p. 80 bottom left

Jet Propulsion Laboratory: p. 22 bottom, pp. 30–31, p. 55 top

Lick Observatory/UC: p. 26, p. 46

Geoffrey McCormack: pp. 4–5, p. 9, p. 10 bottom, pp. 16–17, pp. 18–19, p. 21, p. 23 bottom, p. 24 top, p. 28, p. 29 top, p. 35 left, p. 36 bottom, p. 37, pp. 40–41, p. 43, p. 47 top, p. 47 bottom, pp. 64–65, pp. 66–67, p. 79 top, p. 83, p. 97, p. 98 top

K. Meech/University of Hawaii: p. 94

NASA: p. 14 right, p. 23 top, p. 33 left, p. 33 right, p. 48 top, p. 48 bottom, p. 49, p. 51, p. 53 top, p. 53 bottom, p. 54, p. 55 bottom, p. 56 top, p. 56 bottom, p. 57 bottom, p. 58, p. 59 right, p. 60, p. 61 bottom, pp. 62–63 right, p. 71 top, p. 72 left, p. 72 right, p. 73 left, p. 73 right, p. 75 top right, p. 76, p. 77, p. 78 top, p. 79 bottom, p. 80 top left, p. 80 top right, p. 81 top left, p. 84 bottom, p. 87 top, p. 87 bottom, p. 88, p. 90 top, p. 90 center, p. 90 bottom, p. 91 bottom, p. 92 center, p. 92 bottom, p. 93, p. 103

NASA/Fin-Hol: p. 20, p. 50, p. 70 bottom, p. 75 bottom, p. 82, p. 86 right, p. 102

NASA/David Grinspoon: p. 61 top

NASA/Johnson Space Center: p. 2, p. 3, p. 30 left, p. 33 top, p. 36 top, p. 41 bottom, p. 42, p. 44, p. 45 top, p. 64 inset, p. 69

NASA/JPL: p. 25, p. 35 right, p. 52, p. 75 top left

NASA/JPL/SWRI/Carolyn Porco: p. 68, p. 80 bottom right

NASA/Erich Karkoschka: p. 78 bottom

NASA/NEAR: p. 10 top

NASA/Photri: p. 34, p. 45 bottom, p. 74, p. 81 bottom, p. 85

NASA/SOHO: p. 15

NASA/John Trauger/JPL and James Westphal: p. 11

National Optical Astronomy Observatory: p. 96, p. 100 left

National Space Science Data Center: p. 32, pp. 62–63 left

NOAO/Bill Livingston: p. 14 left

Tory Read: p. 27

M. Rothman: pp. 38–39

J. William Schopf: p. 39

Science Photo Library/Chris Butler: p. 4, p. 95

Space Telescope Science Institute: p. 81 top right

SPL/Lynette Cook: p. 13, p. 59 left

SPL/European Space Agency: p. 12

SPL/David Parker: p. 22 top

Alan Stern & Marc Buie/NASA & ESA: p. 98 bottom

Jason Surace: p. 86 left

United States Naval Observatory: p. 99

Gaylord Welker: p. 84 top

Index